THE SHOOTING SCRIPT

I WENT DOWN

SCREENPLAY AND INTRODUCTION BY
CONOR McPHERSON

NOTES BY
PADDY BREATHNACH, CONOR McPHERSON & ROBERT WALPOLE

N
H
B

The NHB Shooting Script Series

NICK HERN BOOKS

LONDON

The Shooting Script Series was originally devised by Newmarket Press

The Newmarket Shooting Script Series is a registered trademark of Newmarket Press,
a division of Newmarket Publishing Communications Corporation

This book first published in Great Britain and Ireland in 1997
as an original paperback by
Nick Hern Books Ltd, 14 Larden Road, London W3 7ST

A CIP catalogue for this book is available from the British Library

ISBN 1 885459 393 5

Typeset by Country Setting, Woodchurch, Kent TN26 3TB
Printed and bound in Great Britain by Hobbs the Printers Ltd,
Totton, Hants S040 3YS

THE NHB SHOOTING SCRIPT SERIES

The Age of Innocence
I Went Down
The Ice Storm
Jude
The People vs Larry Flynt
The Shawshank Redemption

For information on forthcoming titles, please contact the publishers:
NHB, 14 Larden Road, London W3 7ST

CONTENTS

Above: Peter McDonald as Git Hynes
Below: Antoine Byrne as Sabrina Bradley.

INTRODUCTION
by Conor McPherson

October 1994

I have a play running in the Dublin Theatre Festival called *The Good Thief*. It's about a protection racketeer sent to do a job which goes terribly wrong. He finds himself driving across the country with the wife and three-year-old daughter of a man he was supposed to be intimidating. They are his hostages. They develop an unusual friendship. It all ends in tears.

I get some good reviews. Some of them however feel the play is a meandering macho fantasy which shouldn't be in the theatre. It is suggested that I'm some sort of frustrated screenwriter who can't cut the mustard.

In the audience are the future producer and director of *I Went Down*.

May/June 1995

The Good Thief has just finished a national tour. I've won an award and I feel like a proper playwright.

I read in the *Irish Times* that young Dublin producer Robert Walpole and director Paddy Breathnach have just thrown a hell of a party at the Cannes film festival. For some reason their names stick in my head like a sort of premonition.

A few days later the phone rings. "Hi Conor, my name is Rob Walpole. I'd love to meet you to see if you'd be interested in talking about maybe doing a film project."

We arrange to meet at the Irish Film Centre. I tell Rob he'll recognise me by looking for a guy with red hair and glasses. "I look like a tramp," Rob says.

We meet. First impressions. They're a team. Paddy does the talking. Rob hangs back a little. Supportive. They're practised. They're grown-ups. Paddy is tall, very dark. Considered. I think he's foreign. Rob is shorter, fairer, eager to laugh.

We go for a sandwich. Paddy has just won the San Sebastian film festival with his first feature, *Ailsa*. It's a dark, beautifully atmospheric picture of a man's obsessive love for a woman who moves into the flat below his. It's scripted by Joe O'Connor and has a brilliant lead performance from Brendan Coyle. But now Paddy has decided he'd like to do something more commercial. They think I'm the man.

Paddy produces some photocopied stories, ancient Irish myths. One is called *The Sons of Tuireann*, a revenge story. Paddy thinks it's a good basis for something modern, urban. Irish but universal. Rob gives me a cheque for a hundred quid to go home and see what I think.

I read it and I think it's stupid. People casting spells and turning their enemies into goats and so forth. I don't understand what Paddy wants.

We meet again. "I don't understand what the hell this is about." Paddy frowns. He's not sure either. Rob laughs at Paddy. Paddy laughs at himself. We forget about the myths and I can see I'm going to get on well with this pair.

Over the next few weeks we shoot ideas around for a modern, urban, Irish yet universal story. We don't want to do a film about the North and we don't want to do a film about drugs. It's becoming clear we're probably going to do a film about losers. Rob encourages me to write a treatment, an outline of the film's story, so we can try to raise some development money. I work out some stories, but nobody wants to give us any money. I find writing treatments a bit pointless if no one's going to respond.

I decide to just start writing a script. I decide I don't need any money. I'm on the dole and I'm writing the first draft.

July 1995

I call in to Paddy and Rob's office. We go up to the roof of the building. I read them ten or fifteen pages. I act out all the parts. Some characters are already there who will remain right through to first screening two years later. Christopher 'Git' Hynes, Tom French, Sabrina Bradley, Anto McQuigly, James 'Bunny' Kelly. Paddy and Rob are laughing out loud. I'm a bit thrown. I think it's supposed to be ugly and terrifying. But the characters are *so* concerned with being tough or threatening that their demonstrative natures can't help but reveal their insecurities beneath the surface. There's so much stupid posturing, they verge on being clown-like.

We become intrigued with the idea of having a thriller which can keep you on the edge of your seat and shock you, but still make you burst out laughing. A mixture of suspense and slapstick. We're none of us afraid of genre. We want to play with it. I press ahead, coming in and out every couple of days, going up on the roof, acting it out.

September 1995

My girlfriend gets a job in Leicester. I go and stay with her. While she's out all day I sit and work on the script. I get up to sixty pages. I'm running out of ideas. It's slipping into the darker, more violent areas Paddy wants to avoid. He's concerned we're losing the humour. I'm losing confidence. I finish the draft. It's rushed and patchy. Rob sends the script to various agencies in search of development money. To no avail.

Christmas 1995

I've begun a new draft. I'm keeping it lighter. But I'm feeling daunted. Such a long way to go. Paddy and Rob take me to the Irish Film Ball at Ardmore Studios. Joe O'Connor is accepting an award from Miramax for his screen adaptation of his novel, *Cowboys and Indians*, which he has been developing with Paddy. I drink too much and shoot my mouth off to a journalist without knowing what her job is. I'm quoted in the paper. I'm mortified. I ring Rob. "I'm not sure I can do this." Rob is hungover too. He says, "Conor, the first thirty pages are great. Just give us the other sixty and we'll get the film made, okay?"

Spring 1996

We've sent the second draft out to get some development money. But we don't get any. I need to do something radical. I decide to move into Paddy and Rob's office and write the third draft there while they continue with their other projects, which are popular documentaries, including *The Road to America*, *The Charlton Years* and *WRH*. The phone is ringing. Couriers are coming in and out. I'm chasing the comedy and slimming down the plot. We're out of Dublin. The task is simple. It keeps getting more complicated. I'm testing gags out on whoever's in the office. I try bits of dialogue. It's taking shape. We discuss various endings. We decide on one. I write it and we go to the pub. I want to call it *I Went Down*. They send the script out. Within days the phone is ringing.

Summer 1996

Paddy and Rob are back in Cannes. They ring me in Leicester. The film is financed. Paddy gets ready for preproduction. Casting begins. I'm going to get paid.

Paddy asks some actor friends of mine to read against people who are auditioning. One of my friends is Peter MacDonald. He's reading against assorted Git Hynes's. Paddy's not happy with the people he's seeing, many of whom have already begun successful film careers. Paddy finds himself looking increasingly at

Pete. The Git role is deceptively hard. He's the most reasonable person in the film, so he's the quietest. He's the most solid. He's loyal. He's serious, but he has a sense of humour which we can see without him having to crack jokes. He's our hero and he's in practically every scene. Paddy asks Pete to read as Git. He auditions him about three times. Pete's perfect. He's caught the character's depth where the temptation for others was to play him as a bit of a wideboy chancer. Pete's cast and I'm thrilled.

Brendan Gleeson is cast as Bunny. Pete and Brendan look great together. There's a lot of confidence in the air. With the central double-act in place, Paddy builds the rest of the cast around them.

September 1996

Just before shooting, Paddy asks me to write a scene to get Git and Bunny from a bar into a nightclub. To introduce a nightclub as a location for a scene already written, basically. I decide we should cut to a man walking around a nightclub asking a lot of girls to dance, all of whom refuse him. I feel it'll create a mood of comic sexuality and establish without a doubt just where we are. It's a non-speaking part, played against a background of loud music. Paddy suggests I play it.

Cool.

On the day of my cinematic début our costume designer, Kathy Strachan, shows me my costume. It's a bright red Teddy Boy suit and a black polo-neck sweater. We're shooting the scene at The Kitchen in Dublin. It's packed with extras. The girls I'm asking to dance are lined up. The camera tracks with me while I make my way to the dancefloor, pausing only to proposition women. My hand gestures are those of open surrender. Palms held up as I accept each rejection. We do it six or seven times. I don't want want to go home. I want to run away with the circus.

April/May 1997

With the film completed, me and Paddy and Rob go to the south-eastern states of America to interview sheriffs and federal agents in rural areas. We're researching a film I want to write. This time we've received development money pretty much immediately.

On our return we go to Cannes, where *I Went Down* is having market screenings. I'm walking around in my cheap suit, every inch the screenwriter. At our first screening, the cinema is packed with distributors from all over the world. There's a delay while over a hundred people are turned away. Paddy and Rob are too nervous to watch. As the lights go down I'm wondering if we're going to have a language problem. Will the humour go over? Is everybody just going to get bored?

But once we're into the gags strangers all around me are laughing and applauding. And I know we're okay. In fact I really enjoy it. I like the film.

Later that night we're out celebrating. Distributors are buying it. It's going to be released in every European country, and places all over the world, Australia, New Zealand, Argentina. Someone tells me an Israeli distributor started crying when he was outbid.

I find myself in the company of women. Clutching my drink and swaying. Flushed with success and patting myself on the back, basking in compliments. In a seedy bar. Fit to drop. Paddy grabs me and drags me into the street, out of any potential messing. He shoves me into a taxi. There's a bit of a struggle and Paddy slams the door on my leg, none of which I remember the following morning. I'm walking down the street asking people why I've developed a limp.

And that's the two years I lived with this film. I was doing other things as well, writing plays, getting my mush in the papers and generally making a living. In many ways it was a pain in the arse, and at times I was wondering if it was too much of a drag. But someone told me recently that I should never take for granted what it's like to have a job like this.

It's different.

Conor McPherson
Dublin, August 1997

Peter McDonald as Git Hynes during filming

I WENT DOWN

screenplay by
Conor McPherson

> 'I went down to the Piraeus yesterday
> with Glaucon, the son of Ariston.'
>
> Plato, *The Republic*

1   INT. PRISON VISITING ROOM DAY

A young man in his twenties, GIT sits having a cigarette. SABRINA is led
in. She sits opposite.

> SABRINA
> How are you?

Pause. GIT nods.

> SABRINA
> You got . . . my letter . . .

> GIT
> Yeah.

> SABRINA
> Can you . . . see . . . why?

> GIT
> Well. I knew something was up when
> you, when you weren't coming in.

Pause.

> SABRINA
> Yeah. Well, you know how I feel.
> I can't . . .

> GIT
> I'm sorry.

Pause.

> SABRINA
> You promised me.

> GIT
> I know I did.

Pause.

> SABRINA
> How long do you have?

> GIT
> Another three months.

Pause.

> SABRINA
> Anto feels very guilty. He's still your
> best friend. I need you to tell him you
> think it's okay about me and him.
> When you get out.

Pause.

> GIT
> Is this a joke?

Short pause.

> SABRINA
> No. He can't relax. He thinks . . . either
> I'm going to be back with you, or that
> . . . you're going to go after him.

Short pause.

> GIT
> He knows I wouldn't go after him,
> Sabrina.

> SABRINA
> Just for me, Git. He can't relax. (Pause.)
> I want to give you this.

She takes off a ring.

> SABRINA
> Will you tell him it's okay?

Long pause. GIT regards SABRINA.

MAIN TITLES

2   EXT. PRISON DAY

GIT leaves prison.

3   EXT. STREET DAY

GIT stops at a house and looks at a card.

4   INT. B&B ROOM DAY

GIT puts some clothes in a drawer. He pauses when he finds something in
the bottom of his bag. SABRINA's ring.

5   EXT. TOM FRENCH'S BAR NIGHT

Outside the pub things are quite busy. Not overtly criminal, but someone
exchanges a set of keys. Someone pays someone. Some hangers-on at the
fringes. GIT makes his way into the pub.

GIT comes in. A man, GIT's age, is standing on a little platform, speaking in a microphone. This is GIT's friend ANTO. GIT leans against the bar looking at ANTO.

> ANTO
> You've got to achieve something in
> your life. What the fuck are we doing?
> The jackpot has gone *down* the last two
> weeks. This is your team. We're gonna
> win the league this year. Be part of it.
> Don't be kicking yourself. Come on,
> five for a pound. Look at the prizes for
> fuck's sake!

Laughter. (They don't look too good.) ANTO sees GIT. He loses his confidence a little.

> ANTO
> You can . . . get tickets off me or, at the
> bar.

ANTO puts the microphone away, and moves down off the stage to a table where there are some other men, JOHNNER DOYLE, twenties, sharp, and BUNNY KELLY, thirties, a bit shook.

GIT watches ANTO go over. JOHNNER takes ANTO to one side. JOHNNER seems curt and irritated. ANTO seems to make a discreet appeal. And then GIT is distracted. SABRINA is beside him. They stand together for a moment, not speaking, not even looking at each other, just glances.

> SABRINA
> You okay?

> GIT
> Ah yeah. Bit tired. Just a bit . . . eh.

Pause.

> SABRINA
> Did Anto . . . ? (She nods.) Was he . . .
> (Short pause.)

> GIT
> Ah yeah he, you know. There's no . . .
> I'm . . . It's cool.

> SABRINA
> Have you spoken to him?

> GIT
> Well. I haven't *spoken* to him yet, no.

> SABRINA
> Are you going to?

GIT

Yeah. I'm . . . Who's, who's he with
over there?

SABRINA (looks around)

Tch, ah he's always . . . that's Bunny
Kelly. In the anorak. Used to live
around the corner from me. And I'll
never forget, one Sunday morning,
he had a row with his grand-dad, his
grand-dad, now. And do you know
what he did? He stuck him in the bin.
And everyone was afraid to pull him
out. The poor man was in the bin for
an hour and a half. 'Course he (ANTO)
thinks they're great. Will you go over
to him?

GIT

Yeah. Em. I don't want this.

He shows her the ring.

SABRINA

I don't want it either.

GIT

No it's yours. Whatever about you and
Anto, that has nothing to do with you
and me. (Short pause) So you keep it.
I want you to keep it.

Short pause. He hands her the ring.

GIT

Is that cider?

SABRINA

Yeah. Have you not had a drink yet?

GIT

No. I'm gonna get one now.

SABRINA

Well, let me get this . . . You go and
talk to Anto.

GIT

Okay.

Pause.

SABRINA

Thanks.

She kisses him on the cheek and quickly goes. GIT looks around for
ANTO. He sees BUNNY KELLY sitting alone, then, looking around, he spots
ANTO going through a door with JOHNNER, JOHNNER pushes ANTO.
STEO GANNON, tough looking, pulls the door closed behind them. GIT
looks over at SABRINA who is chatting with some people. He looks at the
door again. He goes over and opens it.

7   INT. CORRIDOR (TOM FRENCH'S BAR) NIGHT.

GIT is in a dark corridor, a chink of light comes from a half-open door.
GIT hears voices and has a look.

8   INT. BACK ROOM (TOM FRENCH'S BAR) NIGHT

The room is an office/storeroom. ANTO is kneeling with his hands held on
a table by STEO. JOHNNER holds a hammer and a pint.

                    JOHNNER
          I'm not particularly fucking interested
          in listening to your financial . . . eh . . .

STEO laughs. He thinks this is a brilliant piece of wit.

                    ANTO
          That's the story Johnner. Just can't get
          it. Just what's coming tonight.

                    JOHNNER
          Well, in my . . . view of it. That's not
          gonna satisfy anybody. You're not even
          making a fucking effort to show any . . .
          that you want to get it sorted out. You
          look like a dozy bollocks.

                    ANTO
          What can I do, but?

                    JOHNNER
          Well. You can get this for a start and
          then we'll take it from there right?

GIT knocks softly on the door.

Pause.

                    JOHNNER
          Hello?

GIT pushes the door open.

                    STEO
          What's the story, Git?

GIT steps into the room a little.

> GIT
>
> How are yous, lads?

> ANTO
>
> Howaya Git.

> JOHNNER
>
> Can I help you there, pal?

> STEO
>
> This is a thing with Anto, Git. We gotta take care of it. He'll be out to yous in a minute.

> GIT
>
> It's just you know. He's wanted now. He has to do the raffle.

> JOHNNER
>
> Excuse me. Would you fuck off please? Thank you.

Pause.

> STEO
>
> I don't wanna have to put you out, Git.

> GIT
>
> I can't go back without him, you know? I mean, I can't do it.

> JOHNNER
>
> Steo . . .

STEO acknowledges this and moves to force GIT out.

> GIT
>
> We got a lot of people outside.

> JOHNNER
>
> They know better.

JOHNNER signals to Steo.

> STEO
>
> I'm putting you out, Git.

> GIT
>
> Okay.

> STEO
>
> Okay?

> GIT
>
> Okay.

> STEO
>
> Okay.

JOHNNER
Jaysus! Steo!

GIT punches STEO. Pause.

STEO
Fucking hell.

GIT hits STEO again, flailing digs over his head. STEO slips and bangs his chin on a table. We hear his teeth bang together. He grunts looking up at JOHNNER confused, and apologetic. JOHNNER shakes his head. Then he smashes his glass, and almost jadedly faces GIT.

JOHNNER
Come on.

> 'This is what I need you to do
> to make it right.'

---

9   INT. TOM FRENCH'S BAR MORNING

It is not open for business. Sunlight streams in. A barman hoovers the floor. In the middle of the floor, GIT and ANTO sit at a table. JOHNNER DOYLE sits to one side, a huge wad of dressing over his left eye. STEO GANNON sits at the bar, one arm in a sling. They are waiting for TOM FRENCH.

GIT and ANTO speak in hushed tones, embarrassed at being in this odd situation.

ANTO
I am really sorry about this.

Pause.

I *never* played before. I thought, I'll
bring fifty quid. I lose it, I lose it. You
know? But that's it I'll never come
back, but you know, all of a sudden,
I'm ahead, you know? And then I lose
a bit, win a bit, lose a bit, borrow a bit.
Borrow a little bit more. Next thing I
know, I'm trying to pay it off. But it had
never gotten heavy like that before. I
swear to God. You saved me there you
know?

GIT's impatient look is telling ANTO to shut up.

ANTO
I'm gonna explain everything. Just
leave it to me. Okay?

Pause. GIT just looks at ANTO. TOM FRENCH comes into the room.

> ANTO
>
> Okay?

TOM FRENCH is in his fifties, heavy set, wears a suit. He sits at the table, opposite GIT and ANTO. He considers GIT for a moment.

> TOM
>
> I remember when I was your age.

Pause.

> TOM
>
> I was probably worse than you. I was a little bollix. Oh yeah. I was the one knacker you didn't want to come near. Forget it. Forget about it. But I was never stupid. And you've been very fuckin' stupid.

> ANTO
>
> He made a mistake Mr. French. he didn't know the score.

> TOM
>
> Anto, I appreciate what you're doing. And you're shitting your pants. You don't know what's gonna happen. And that's probably good sense. But at the end of the day, you're an arsehole. And you're the last person I'm gonna listen to. You know what I mean? So shut up. Because if I think you're getting a smart mouth, I'll kick your head in. Alright?

ANTO nods. TOM nods back.

> TOM (addressing GIT)
>
> Now you! I'm talking to you, Rocky Five.

GIT finally looks at him. TOM indicates JOHNNER.

> TOM
>
> Look at his face.

GIT looks only at FRENCH.

> If you don't look at him, I'll break your fucking legs.

GIT looks at the table and then finally up at JOHNNER who sits ashamed.

                    TOM
        He lost the eye. You destroyed his face.
        What kind of horrible, ugly, desperate
        bitch is he gonna end up with?

GIT looks at the table.

                    TOM
        He'll be lucky if some Arab lets him
        finger his dog's arse for a fiver.

ANTO smirks.

                    TOM
        You like that, do you?

                    ANTO
        It's just, you know, the way you said it
        was funny.

                    TOM
        Steo, take him inside, put Sky . . .
        Sport . . . on the . . .

                    ANTO
        I'm sorry, I won't say anything.

STEO comes over.

                    TOM
        I'm finished with you anyway. This is
        between me and him now.

ANTO gets up heavily.

                    ANTO
        I'll wait for you.

GIT nods, and STEO brings ANTO out. TOM signals to JOHNNER to
leave also.

                    TOM
        Now, by rights, and normally there is
        no fucking way I'd be sitting here even
        discussing this, I would've had your
        eye. (Pause.) He's my sister's boy.
        I think he's useless. But I can't have
        this. I can't have her hanging out of
        me bollocks. Tryna get me to do
        something. (Pause.) Do you know who
        Frank Grogan is?

                    GIT
        No.

TOM produces a photo, slides it across to GIT.

                              TOM
                    Old associate of mine. He was down in
                    Cork doing a deal for me. Johnner was
                    supposed to go down and pick up the
                    money. But obviously he couldn't,
                    because he can't even . . . see now. I
                    would have had another fella do it, but
                    he's doing eight months for contempt.
                    And that Steo is useless. Grogan hasn't
                    got in touch with me. I reckon he's
                    panicked. He thinks something's up. I
                    need someone to go and find him.
                    Bring the money back.

Pause.

                              GIT
                    Mr. French, I'm only out of prison. It's
                    very difficult for me to get involved in
                    anything like this.

Pause.

                              TOM
                    There won't be any problems. All I
                    want you to do is pick someone up at
                    three o'clock in Gort and take him
                    down to Grogan. A friendly face. To
                    help him out. Reassure him. This is an
                    easy ride for you. Johnner handled it
                    very badly. But this is what I need you
                    to do to make it right.

                              GIT
                    Jesus, Mr. French. I'd like to help and
                    get this all outta the way, but it was an
                    accident. And I'm, you know . . .

                              TOM
                    Well, if you don't wanna do it, don't.
                    Just give me twenty-five thousand
                    pounds and I won't be outta pocket.

Pause. GIT looks away. TOM hands GIT an envelope.

                              TOM
                    This is details of where Frank has been
                    the last few days. Keep the photo.

Pause. GIT gets up.

                              GIT
                    I'll see if Anto can get us a car.

Short pause.

                               12

> TOM (shakes his head)
> I think Anto should stay here.

> GIT
> What, *here*, here?

> TOM
> Sooner you get back, sooner he can go.
> (Laughs.) Don't worry, you've got
> company.

> GIT
> Who?

10   EXT. TOM FRENCH'S BAR MORNING

GIT and TOM stand in the carpark. A new car (Car A) pulls in. It is driven by BUNNY KELLY. GIT reacts a little.

> GIT
> Bunny . . . ?

> TOM (waves)
> Kelly's a good man. I don't think you'll
> have any problems. Bitta co-operation.
> He fucks up, it's *your* fault. You fuck
> up, it's his. That way I don't have to go
> around *trusting* everybody.

11   INT. CAR A DAY

BUNNY drives. Doesn't seem interested in GIT.

12   EXT. SUBURBAN STREET DAY

The car pulls up outside a house.

13   INT. CAR A DAY

> BUNNY
> I just gotta nip in here for a sec.

14   EXT. BUNNY'S DAY

BUNNY tries a key in the door. It doesn't work. He looks at it. Pause. He tries it again. It doesn't work. He rings the bell. No answer. He rings again and knocks. No answer. He goes around the side of the house.

15   INT. CAR A DAY

GIT sees classical music tapes on the floor. He opens the envelope TOM FRENCH gave him. There is a sheet of paper with a few addresses and a hand-drawn map. GIT looks at the photo TOM gave him. The photo shows people at a wedding. A YOUNG TOM FRENCH, a YOUNG FRANK GROGAN and another, older man, SONNY MULLIGAN. Seventies fashions. FRANK GROGAN's face is ringed in pen.

16   EXT. BACK OF BUNNY'S HOUSE DAY

BUNNY is looking in a window with his hands to the glass.

> BUNNY
> This is stupid. Number one, I can see
> you. Number two, you're moving, and
> number three, I . . . know you're in
> there. I can see you. You're behind
> the couch. I can see you. Are you
> gonna let me in? (Pause.) I can't talk
> through this.

Long pause. Some CHILDREN from next door look over the wall at him. He sees them. Pause. He turns back to the window.

> BUNNY
>
> Teresa.

17   EXT. COUNTRY ROAD DAY

The car speeds along.

18   INT. CAR A DAY

GIT cannot help looking down at the pair of white dressy shoes that BUNNY wears.

> GIT
> Do you know who this friendly . . . face
> is?

> BUNNY
>
> No.

> GIT
> D'you know Grogan?

> BUNNY (lighting a cigarette)
> I know of him.

> GIT
>
> Yeah?

> BUNNY
> Yeah. He's one a these older . . . you
> know, knocking around in the old days.
> Him and Tom French woulda worked
> with Sonny Mulligan and that. Getting
> up to all sorts of . . . you know . . . But
> I didn't think him and French were still
> buds. Bit surprised.

14

                    GIT
Says here . . . he was staying at the
Glenwood hotel.

                    BUNNY
Okay.

                    GIT
But that's outta the picture. There's no
way he's still gonna be there . . .

                    BUNNY
I don't know. If that's where he's
staying . . .

                    GIT
But if he doesn't know what's going on.
He'll be moving around, you know?

Pause.

                    BUNNY
Well that's one theory.

Pause.

                    GIT
Why would he stay in the same place?

                    BUNNY
Why wouldn't he?

                    GIT
He'd want to keep the head down. He
doesn't know what's after happening.
Play it safe.

                    BUNNY
Ah, he's an old time . . . fella, you
know? I'd say he'd be calm about the
whole thing.

                    GIT
Yeah. I'm not saying the man's not
calm. I'm saying he's not gonna stay
where any idiot can find him.

                    BUNNY
Yeah. I know what you're saying. But
what are you basing this on?

                    GIT
What do you mean?

                    BUNNY
I mean, what are you basing your
opinion on?

                    GIT
Because it's what I'd do.

                    BUNNY
But you're not him, are you? D'you see
what I'm saying. About an open mind
to these things? I'm not trying to say
anything. Don't get me wrong. This is
not about you. I don't know you. But
I've got to go on what I do know.

                    GIT
What do you mean?

                    BUNNY
I mean, you're a young guy . . .

                    GIT
Oh, right, so you're . . .

                    BUNNY
Don't get me wrong. I'm not blaming
you for your opinions. That's what you
do. Fine. I'm not saying that. But
there's a little more experience on my
side that might help us to get the job
done that bit quicker, alright? Just pick
up this friendly face. He knows
Grogan. See what he says.

                    GIT
So what do you want to do?

Pause.

                    BUNNY
I wanna, I think I wanna see when we
get there. Do you see what I'm saying?

                    GIT
See when we get there.

                    BUNNY
That's the plan.

19   EXT. PETROL STATION DAY

This is the middle of nowhere. They pull in.

20   INT. CAR DAY

BUNNY hands GIT some money.

16

> BUNNY
> Get me some fags, will you?

GIT looks at the money, unhappy at having to run this type of errand.

> BUNNY
> And get us something to eat.

Pause.

> What are you waiting for?

GIT gets out.

21   INT. PETROL STATION SHOP

GIT comes in. An ATTENDANT works behind the counter, he is middle-aged.

> ATTENDANT
> Hello, how are you?

> GIT
> How's it going?

> ATTENDANT
> Not too bad a day now.

> GIT
> No.

GIT is looking at crisps, selecting packets, soft drinks. He sees a payphone and goes to it. He dials.

> MAN'S VOICE
> Hello?

> GIT
> Hello. Is Sabrina there please?

Pause.

> SABRINA
> Hello?

> GIT
> Hiya, it's Git.

Pause.

> SABRINA
> Is everything okay?

> GIT
> Yeah. You?

> SABRINA
> Mm hm. Where are you?

17

Pause.

>   GIT
> I'm eh, just, me and Anto are heading
> down the country . . . for the day. He
> just asked me to give you a quick buzz.

Pause.

>   SABRINA
> Will you put him on?

>   GIT
> Eh, he's filling the car up.

>   SABRINA
> What car?

Short pause.

>   GIT
> That I borrowed off a bloke this
> morning.

Long pause.

>   GIT
> So how are you? Okay, yeah?

>   SABRINA
> Yeah. I'm alright.

Pause.

>   GIT
> Well, I'll get Anto to give you a buzz,
> later, yeah?

>   SABRINA
> Yeah, okay.

>   GIT
> Okay. See you soon.

GIT hangs up, keeps his hand on the receiver for a moment. Eyes closed.
He gets himself together, picks up the crisps etc., and goes to the
ATTENDANT.

>   GIT
> Right eh . . . these and . . . twenty
> Major, and eh . . . (Indicates BUNNY at
> the car.) whatever that is.

THE ATTENDANT rings up the items.

>   ATTENDANT (a little laugh)
> He hasn't put anything in it yet.

GIT

What?

GIT looks out the window and sees BUNNY having trouble with the petrol cap.

23   EXT. PETROL STATION DAY

GIT comes out to BUNNY. BUNNY is trying to open the petrol cap with a small knife.

GIT

What's the story?

BUNNY

What's it look like?

GIT sees classical music albums on the back seat.

GIT

It looks like you stole this car.

BUNNY

Yup. You go on in and get the fags and that, and I'll have this off in a minute.

GIT

He's only waiting on this.

BUNNY

Well, I'll tell you what, it's not helping anybody you standing there looking at me. Keeping the pressure on, now, is it?

GIT

I'm not trying to put pressure on you. Just he's looking at us (GIT gives the attendant a little wave.) and he's gonna twig any second that this is not our car.

BUNNY

Because do you ever remember when you were young and you could never do anything right when someone was watching you?

Pause.

GIT

What?

BUNNY

Press in here.

GIT

Where?

19

> BUNNY
> Here. All around the rim. Yeah. Press in
> hard. Now . . .

BUNNY continues to work and the petrol cap pops out.

> BUNNY
> Right, you fill that up.

GIT gets the nozzle and BUNNY goes into the shop. GIT fills the tank, looking around, a little nervous now that he knows the car is stolen. He finishes and jams the petrol cap back in as best he can. He turns around. No sign of BUNNY. GIT begins to go towards the shop.

24   INT. PETROL STATION SHOP DAY

GIT comes in and is shocked to see BUNNY on the other side of the counter emptying the till.

> GIT
> What are you doing?

> BUNNY
> Come here and give me a hand.

> GIT (going to counter)
> Where's your man?

> BUNNY
> He's down here.

GIT looks down. The ATTENDANT is on the floor with masking tape round his hands, ankles and mouth. BUNNY holds a small revolver trained on the ATTENDANT.

> GIT
> Oh . . . *Fuck*!

> BUNNY
> Take this! Come on take it!

He hands GIT the gun.

> BUNNY
> Cover him.

BUNNY goes in the back.

> GIT
> Where are you going?

BUNNY does not answer.

> GIT (annoyed)
> Oh, *bollix*!

24A   INT. PETROL STATION POV CLOSED CIRCUIT SECURITY CAMERA

GIT looks down at the ATTENDANT. The ATTENDANT is helpless and
terrified. GIT does not want this situation but he finds resolve and
commits himself.

> GIT
> If you move, I'll kill you.

The camera goes dead.

24B   INT. PETROL STATION

BUNNY comes back. He carries a video tape. They make their way out.

> BUNNY
> Had to get them.

He indicates upwards. GIT looks up and sees the security cameras.

25   EXT. PETROL STATION DAY

GIT and BUNNY come out to the car. BUNNY is dropping chocolate bars
from a pile he holds to his chest. They get in and drive away, just as
another car pulls into the station.

26   INT. CAR A DAY

They drive in silence. GIT is furious. He keeps his hand up to his face
looking out the window. BUNNY glances at GIT. Seeing that it will be bad
policy to carry on like this.

> BUNNY
> Clocked us messing with the cap. He
> knew the car was hot. Woulda shopped
> us in a minute. Had to do it. (Pause.)
> Had to be done.

Pause.

> GIT
> Did you have to rob the place?

Pause. BUNNY has no answer. GIT is right. But it was just natural
for BUNNY.

> BUNNY
> Have to dump the car.

GIT glares at BUNNY.

27   EXT. COUNTRYSIDE DAY

GIT and BUNNY walk through a field with some cows (BUNNY regards
them suspiciously), odd figures in this setting, dressed for the city in the
middle of nowhere. Smoking cigarettes.

21

                              GIT
            Could we not have waited till the next
            town, no?

                              BUNNY
            Nah, fuck that. Stay on that road too
            long, where you gonna go? Cops see
            you, you're snared rapid.

It starts to rain. GIT turns and looks at BUNNY.

                         BUNNY (pause)
            I don't wanna hear it, right? I'm just . . .
            I don't even wanna hear it.

BUNNY walks on. GIT watches him, then flicks his cigarette away and
follows.

28   EXT. STREET IN A SMALL RURAL TOWN DAY

GIT stands on the street, having a cigarette. A filthy battered old car (Car B)
chugs around the corner. BUNNY is driving. GIT is horrified. BUNNY stops
and leans across opening the passenger door. GIT gets in.

29   EXT. ROAD DAY

The car is stopped at the side of the road. BUNNY has the bonnet open
and leans into the engine. GIT sits behind the wheel.

                              BUNNY
            Try it now.

GIT turns it over. The car does not start. BUNNY slams the bonnet and
comes to GIT's window.

                              BUNNY
            You eh, you don't know anything about
            engines, do you?

                              GIT
            Afraid not, no.

                              BUNNY
            Okay. Well you're gonna have to give it
            a push.

Pause. GIT just looks at BUNNY.

                              GIT
            Excuse me?

                              BUNNY
            Come on, we don't have all day.

                         GIT
          Yeah, well, you know, I'll tell you what,
          I probably wouldn't do it properly, you
          know what I mean? I'd probably only
          fuck it up. So why don't you push the
          fucking car?

GIT rolls up the window.

30   INT. CAR B OPEN ROAD DAY

They drive in silence. GIT is looking at the photograph of the man they are
supposed to find. He smiles up at GIT. The atmosphere is still very frosty
between him and BUNNY. They are wet.

                        BUNNY
          Can you get that heater on?

GIT fiddles with the heater, it makes a strange farting noise and emits a
smell which GIT and BUNNY react to.

                        BUNNY
          Oh Jesus. (Short pause.) Oh Jesus,
          that's disgusting. Turn it off. Turn it off!

GIT turns it off.

                         GIT
          Not *my* fault . . .

Pause. GIT looks at his watch.

                         GIT
          We're gonna miss this guy.

                        BUNNY
          Who?

                         GIT
          The friendly face.

                    BUNNY (short pause)
          'The friendly face . . . '

They chug along. BUNNY tries the radio. Nothing but static with very faint
overlapping signals.

                        BUNNY
          For fuck's sake. (Then looking in
          the rear-view mirror.) Ah no . . . Ah
          Jesus . . .

GIT looks around as a sensible little hatchback driven by two nuns easily
overtakes them. GIT smiles to himself, enjoying BUNNY'S discomfort.

                              BUNNY
              Fucking nuns. (Pause.) Is there any
              chocolate left?

                      GIT (looks for some)
        No.

                              BUNNY
              Is there none left?

                      GIT (pause)
        I don't eat chocolate.

                      BUNNY (pause)
        Well, I've got to eat.

GIT looks at him.

                              BUNNY
              I have a little condition.

31   EXT. LANDSCAPE SHOT OF BOG

31A   EXT. BOGLAND DAY

      The car is parked. Across some marshy land there is an old garage,
      closed, run down. Near the garage is a small caravan.

32   EXT. BOG DAY

      GIT and BUNNY walk towards the garage. BUNNY is eating a sandwich.
      He is a little ahead of GIT. GIT is reading the map and falls into a watery
      hole.

                              GIT
              Jesus! Bunny!

                              BUNNY
              What are you doing?

                              GIT
              I can't feel the bottom!

                              BUNNY
              For fuck's sake.

      BUNNY hesitates and then takes a bite of his sandwich before throwing it
      away. He then helps GIT out of the hole.

                              BUNNY
              I'm gonna ruin my shoes.

33   EXT. GARAGE EARLY EVENING

      It doesn't look like this garage has been open in years. GIT tries the door,
      locked. A sign creaks in the wind.

                               24

BUNNY bangs on the side.

> BUNNY
> Hello?

GIT joins him. GIT sees a piece of paper under a brick. He picks it up.

> GIT
> 'Couldn't wait any more.'

> BUNNY
> Is that it?

> GIT
> We've fucked this up. Fucking car . . .

> BUNNY
> Don't worry about it. We'll get Grogan.
> We don't need this cunt. But I'll tell you
> something. Blaming people's not worth
> the paper it's written on.

BUNNY walks away. GIT watches him. Then follows.

> GIT
> What are you talking about? How are
> we gonna get him?

> BUNNY
> We'll get him.

> GIT
> We need the friendly face.

> BUNNY
> I'm getting a bit tired of hearing about
> this friendly fucking face. Why don't
> you use your initiative, and stop acting
> like a fucking baby.

> GIT
> If we mess this up, Tom French is
> gonna eat us.

BUNNY reaches the car.

> BUNNY
> No guts, no black pudding. And I think
> you know what I'm talking about.

> GIT (short pause)
> That's not an argument.

> BUNNY
> Stay here and be a boy then. The men
> are getting in the car.

35   INT. CAR B DAY

Music is playing. GIT and BUNNY are not too comfortable, wet. A few little
bits where we see them catching each other looking at each other. BUNNY
tries eating a sandwich while driving. Drops it on his lap etc. GIT looking
at GROGAN'S photo. BUNNY flirts with two girls in another car, but they
are more interested in GIT.

36   EXT. GLENWOOD HOTEL DAY

BUNNY comes out and goes to the car. GIT sits in the car.

37   INT. CAR B EARLY EVENING

BUNNY starts the car.

                         BUNNY
              He checked out yesterday. Gotta start
              somewhere. First rule.

GIT takes out the envelope.

                          GIT
              There's a pub he drinks in. Someone
              mighta seen him.

38   EXT. STREET EARLY EVENING

The car pulls up near a pub, GIT gets out.

39   INT. CAR B EARLY EVENING

                          GIT
              You not coming in?

                         BUNNY
              Let's not draw loads of attention to
              ourselves like a pair of fucking clowns,
              okay? I'll see you when you're finished
              wasting all our fucking time, alright?
              I'm gonna get a room. Long drive.

40   EXT. STREET EARLY EVENING

GIT gets out. BUNNY drives away.

41   INT. CORK BAR EARLY EVENING

A small bar in the city. It is dark with only one or two DRINKERS sitting in
the shadows. A bit unsettling. A lone BARMAN leans back against the till,
arms folded looking down. A sense of duty from him. A poor reception
on the radio, the shipping forecast. GIT enters and takes the place in.
He goes to the bar and sits on a stool. The BARMAN looks up.

                              GIT
                    Howaya, eh, pint of eh . . . Murphy's
                    please.

The BARMAN begins to work. GIT is annoyed at how odd the place is, not
sound. He pulls the photo out.

                              GIT
                    I don't know if you can help me . . . I'm
                    looking for a friend of mine. I was
                    supposed to meet him in here a few
                    days ago. Wondering if you'd seen
                    him.

The BARMAN pauses and finally takes the photo.

                              GIT
                    He's the one on the left.

The BARMAN looks at it and hands it back. No reaction.

                              GIT
                    Was he in?

The BARMAN nods and places GIT's pint on the bar.

                            BARMAN
                    That's one sixty-seven.

                              GIT
                    Yeah.

He counts change out of his pocket.

                              GIT
                    When was he in?

                            BARMAN
                    Few days ago.

There is loads more to this than meets the eye. GIT knows this. Pause.
GIT nods.

                              GIT
                    Few days ago, yeah?

The BARMAN nods. Pause.

                              GIT
                    Did he leave a message? D'you know
                    where he is?

The BARMAN stares at GIT and then turns to a phone on the wall. He
pushes two buttons. We do not hear what he says. The BARMAN nods,
looking at GIT. Then he hangs up.

                            BARMAN
                    There'll be someone down now.

                              GIT
          Who?

                            BARMAN
          Someone who can help you.

Pause. The BARMAN continues to work. A door opens further down the
bar. A figure stands in the doorway. The light is behind them, we cannot
see who this is. Pause.

                             VOICE
          You looking for Frank?

Long pause.

                              GIT
          D'you know where he is?

                             VOICE
          He's in here.

Pause.

                              GIT
          He's here?

                             VOICE
          Yeah, come on, he's waiting for you.

42   EXT. STREET EVENING

BUNNY sits in the car looking at a paperback western. He is startled by a
knocking at the window. GIT stands there with blood streaming down his
face. He collapses against the car.

┌─────────────────────────────────────┐
│   'Attentive care and advice.   │
│   Some reconnaissance. Instruction   │
│   in firearms. A daring rescue!'   │
└─────────────────────────────────────┘

43   INT. HOTEL ROOM NIGHT

A cheap room. GIT sits in a chair, head back. His nose is broken. BUNNY
attempts to reset it. Agony. BUNNY appraises his work, hands GIT a small
mirror. GIT has a look.

                            BUNNY
          If it's not right, it's worth tryna do it
          now. You'll never get it right later.

                          GIT (pause)
          Go again.

                               28

                    BUNNY (working on GIT's face)
          These fuckers must have Grogan. (Pause.) We
          have to try and find him.

                    GIT
          We could tip the guards off.

                    BUNNY
          They musta dislodged your brain, did
          they? We get the guards involved, drag
          Tom French into this, he'll go fucking
          spare. Whatever you owe him now will
          seem like nothing when he's finished
          with you. We gotta do this. How's that?

GIT looks in the mirror.

                    BUNNY
          This might sound mad. But I think you
          look better than you used to, d'you
          know what I mean?

BUNNY takes a bag and hands it to GIT.

                    BUNNY
          Here.

GIT takes the bag. Inside is a coat.

                    BUNNY
          Saw you didn't have one.

                    GIT
          Didn't get time to pick it up. How much
          do I owe you?

                    BUNNY
          Get me next time.

45   EXT. STREET WITH BAR NIGHT

46   INT. CAR B NIGHT

GIT and BUNNY sit in the car watching the bar.

                    GIT
          What's the story? You and French.
          (Pause.)

                    BUNNY
          Suits me, to do this.

                    GIT
          What is it? Debt?

                            29

BUNNY
> Yeah. A debt.

GIT
> Yeah?

They sit in silence. The lights of the bar go off. The BARMAN comes out and locks up.

BUNNY
> That him?

GIT
> Mmm.

They watch the BARMAN go to his car and drive away. BUNNY starts up.

47   INT. CAR B CITY STREETS NIGHT

They follow him at a distance. Through the city. Always a few cars behind.

48   EXT. COUNTRYSIDE NIGHT

The BARMAN's car drives through the countryside. GIT and BUNNY follow.

49   INT. CAR B NIGHT

They can see the BARMAN's car, which is just his faint tail-lights far ahead. Very dark. The tail-lights turn off into driveway.

BUNNY
> Aye, aye.

They pull over and look up a slight incline to where the BARMAN is parking. A modern house in the middle of the countryside. There are a few lights on. BUNNY drives on.

50   INT. CAR B NIGHT

They stop in a very quiet place. BUNNY shuts the engine off. GIT gets out.

51   EXT. COUNTRYSIDE NIGHT

GIT goes across a small field. He comes to a stream. He attempts to jump it and falls in. He climbs back out and goes into a clump of trees. He can see the lights of the house. He runs towards it, crouching.

52   EXT. HOUSE NIGHT

GIT goes to a window and has a look. The BARMAN is putting some food from a pot on to a plate. He takes a can of beer and carries a tray from the room.

30

GIT goes round the house to another room. Through a chink in the curtains, he can see a group of men sitting around, playing cards and drinking. One of the men GIT recognises as FRANK GROGAN. GROGAN is not playing cards, he sits alone on a chair. GIT has a quick look at the photo to confirm that this is him. GIT is startled by bottles being knocked over. He looks down to see the glowing eyes of a black cat looking up at him. He looks back into the room. One of the men at the table gets up and stretches. He takes a shotgun from the corner and leaves the room. GIT runs away from the house. As he reaches the clump of trees, the door of the house opens and the man with the shotgun comes out and looks around.

53   EXT. CAR B NIGHT

GIT reaches the car and gets in. BUNNY isn't there. GIT looks around and gets back out.

                    GIT (a whisper)
            Bunny? Bunny?

A hand comes out from beneath the car and grabs GIT's ankle. GIT gets a shock.

                    GIT
            Oh Jesus!

                    BUNNY (from beneath the car)
            Cool it, it's me . . .

BUNNY crawls out.

                    GIT
            What are you doing?

                    BUNNY
            Had to make sure it was you.

54   EXT. A FOREST EARLY MORNING

GIT and BUNNY are in quite a desolate area. It is misty. They are a bit cold. BUNNY and GIT drink tea from take-away polystyrene cups. BUNNY is crouched down with a bag, he takes out two objects wrapped in cloth. He puts one in his pocket and unwraps the other, a small revolver.

                    BUNNY
            You ever used one before?

GIT shakes his head.

                    BUNNY
            D'you know anything about them?

                    GIT
            No, never . . . never used one.

                    BUNNY
          What were you in prison for?

                      GIT
          Indecent exposure.

                    BUNNY
          Were you?

                      GIT
          No I wasn't! Come on, show me.

                    BUNNY
          Take it.

GIT takes it, feeling its weight.

                    BUNNY
          Heavier than you thought it was gonna
          be . . .

                      GIT
          Fucking right.

                    BUNNY
          Right, it's not loaded, right? So, it's
          safe. But when it is loaded, you can't
          be too careful. So we always leave one
          chamber empty.

GIT looks blankly at the gun. BUNNY takes it and opens it.

                    BUNNY
          The holes where the bullets go, they're
          called chambers, right?

                      GIT
          Right.

                    BUNNY
          Now I'm gonna load it. See, you pull
          this, and this part comes out and now
          you can put the bullets in.

BUNNY puts the bullets in.

                    BUNNY
          Now, you see I'm only putting in five?
          You see that? The gun *takes* six.

                      GIT
          Six-shooter.

                    BUNNY
          So one of the chambers is empty.

32

                              GIT

Okay.

                             BUNNY

And that's the one we leave under the
hammer. You see? When I close the
gun, this, this is the hammer. That's
what hits the bullet and the gun goes
off. So, what it is, if the gun gets
jostled, we don't leave a bullet in that
chamber. The hammer's on an empty
chamber

                              GIT

Okay.

                             BUNNY

And then when you pull the trigger
back like this, this bit goes around and
now there's a chamber with a bullet.
The gun is cocked and it's ready to fire.

                              GIT

And the thing goes round.

                             BUNNY

Yeah. Yeah, you want rapid fire you got
to 'fan' the hammer with the palm of
your hand, like this.

BUNNY makes a back-and-forward motion with his open palm. Then he
hands the gun to GIT.

                             BUNNY

I mean, that's an old gun, but, you
know, it's in good nick. But, it's old, it's
been around. You don't wanna get
caught with it, they'll do you for nearly
every job since 1977.

They laugh.

                              GIT

I was six.

                             BUNNY

So. But, seriously, every time you fire
it, it becomes more identifiable. So,
you know, to make it worth my while
keeping it. Every time you fire it . . .
you owe me . . . a hundred quid
alright? Is that fair?

                              GIT

It's not part of the job?

                    BUNNY
          The 'job'? No way, son. Independent
          operators. Best way not to get involved.
          There's nothing like a financial
          arrangement to help people keep a bit
          of distance. That's the way. (Short
          pause.) Okay, show me how you're
          gonna use it.

                    GIT
          What, shoot it?

                    BUNNY
          No, use it. You know, you're going in
          with these fellas, what are you gonna
          do with it?

                    GIT
          You know . . . show them I mean
          business. You know . . .

He points it a little bit.

                    BUNNY
          Well, yeah, I mean, that's the *idea*. But
          you've got to use it to your advantage,
          you know? You've got to use
          everything you've got, give you the
          edge.

BUNNY suddenly pulls his own gun out of his pocket. It is considerably
larger than GIT's revolver. He points it directly at GIT's face, pushing him
down on the ground.

                    BUNNY (screaming)
          Get-down-on-the-fucking-floor-I'll-
          burst-your-fucking-head-open-you-
          little-cunt-you-move-I'll-blow-your-
          fucking-head-off!

He puts his foot on GIT's head. GIT lies in the muck, still holding the cups
of tea without spillage, oddly sedate.

                    BUNNY
          D'you hear me? Do you? Do you?

                    GIT
          Yeah.

BUNNY is immediately calm. He helps GIT up.

                    BUNNY (a little laugh)
          Y'alright?

                    GIT
          Yeah.

                    BUNNY
        See, gun's no use unless you point it,
        and it's no use pointing it unless you
        make them believe you're just about
        fucked up to use it.

                    GIT
        I think you *are* fucked up.

                    BUNNY
        These'll help as well.

BUNNY produces two balaclavas. One is a standard black mask with eye
holes and a gap for the mouth. But the one he hands GIT is a brown
helmet balaclava which reveals the face, hiding the neck and ears.
GIT puts it on.

                    BUNNY
        I could only get one cool one. That one
        is one my nephew had.

55   INT. HOUSE MORNING

      This is the house GIT was looking at last night. All is quiet. One man sits
      with the shotgun at the kitchen table. He has fallen asleep.

56   EXT. HOUSE MORNING

      GIT and BUNNY wear their balaclavas and look in the kitchen window.
      GIT also wears a scarf. They move to the back door. GIT carefully slides
      his hand through the catflap. BUNNY pokes a rod through the keyhole.

57   INT. KITCHEN MORNING

      The key in the door jiggles.

58   EXT. DOOR MORNING

      BUNNY continues to work. It seems to take a long time. GIT looks up at
      BUNNY. BUNNY stops working and looks at GIT,

                    BUNNY (whispers)
        Stop looking at me.

      Pause. GIT looks away, shaking his head.

59   INT. KITCHEN MORNING

      The key jiggles out more but hangs in the keyhole.

60   EXT. DOOR MORNING

      BUNNY looks down at GIT. GIT shrugs, he hasn't felt the key. BUNNY
      begins to gently shake the door.

61   INT. KITCHEN MORNING

The key dangles in the keyhole and drops into GIT's hand.

62   INT. HOUSE MORNING

GIT and BUNNY sneak into the kitchen. GIT carefully moves the shotgun away and BUNNY puts his hand over the man's mouth. The man wakes up and struggles. BUNNY thumps him with his revolver. They hold him on the ground and BUNNY puts masking tape around his mouth. They secure his hands and ankles, taping him to the chair.

63   INT. HALLWAY MORNING

GIT and BUNNY move silently through the house. The living room is empty, just the remains of last night's card game. They look into one of the bedrooms. A man snores in bed. BUNNY looks at GIT. GIT shakes his head. They go into another bedroom. A man sleeps with his head turned towards the wall. GIT sneaks over to the bed, leaning on the wall to get a look at the man's face. He then turns and nods at BUNNY pointing at the man. It is FRANK GROGAN. BUNNY nods.

63A   INT. HALLWAY MORNING

BUNNY watches a man sleeping in a room across the hallway. GIT gently wakes FRANK. FRANK's eyes open.

64   INT. BEDROOM MORNING

> GIT
> It's okay, you're safe now.

> FRANK
> What?

> GIT
> You're safe.

Pause. FRANK looks at GIT's weird garb.

> FRANK
> Is this a dream?

> GIT
> No, it's real. We're gonna take you
> back. Is the money here?

> FRANK
> What money?

> GIT
> The money from the deal.

> FRANK
> I don't know.

GIT
Come on, we'll get you up.

GIT gets GROGAN up, brings him to the hallway.

65   INT. HALLWAY MORNING

BUNNY
Where's the money?

An alarm clock goes off in the room where BUNNY was watching the man sleeping. BUNNY and GIT flash a look at each other. BUNNY throws GROGAN to GIT. GIT holds him. BUNNY goes to the man in bed.

66   INT. BEDROOM MORNING

BUNNY (shouting)
Down! Stay fucking down you culchie
bollocks! I'll blow your fucking head
off. Come on. On the floor!

The man complies.

67   INT. HALLWAY MORNING.

Another man, the BARMAN appears at a bedroom door. GIT turns, pointing the gun at him, joining in the shouting.

GIT
Get down on the floor! Down now!
Down!

The BARMAN crawls into the bedroom, lies on the floor.

BUNNY
Now you boys stay down, we start
shooting!

GIT pushes GROGAN into the hallway.

68   EXT. HOUSE MORNING

GIT and BUNNY bring GROGAN out the house in his pyjamas and bare feet. They go across the grass, BUNNY turning and pointing his gun at the house.

FRANK
Where are yous bringing me?

GIT (reassuringly)
Back up to Tom French.

FRANK (resisting, then lying down)
What? No. No.

37

GIT
What are you doing?

The CORK MEN are shooting from the house. BUNNY returns fire. BUNNY thumps FRANK over the head. FRANK gets weak. They pick him up and carry him.

69   EXT. WOODS MORNING

They get GROGAN to where they have stashed the car. GIT goes around and opens the boot. BUNNY brings GROGAN to the boot. They pause, peering into the squalid mess, muck and what looks suspiciously like a pile of shit.

GIT
What the fuck is that?

BUNNY (shrugs)
Sorry, Frank.

They drop FRANK into the boot.

70   INT. CAR B MORNING

GIT
This is bollocksed. He didn't want to come with us.

BUNNY
You didn't get the money.

GIT
Says he doesn't know anything about it. Bunny, he nearly died when I said Tom French.

Pause.

BUNNY
I'm telling you. (Short pause.) If he's nicked it, he can face the music. It's not our fault. (Pause.) I've had a feeling about this. You know?

GIT looks at BUNNY.

71   EXT. PHONE BOX DAY

The car is parked. GIT and BUNNY are in the box. Both holding the receiver.

GIT
He didn't want to come with us.

72   INT. TOM FRENCH'S BAR DAY

JOHNNER is on the phone. TOM FRENCH is nearby.

> JOHNNER
> Well of course he didn't want to go
> with yous. 'Cause you made a mess of
> it and you never got Frank's pal, did
> you?

73   INT. PHONE BOX

> GIT (pause)
> We had a few problems and we got
> delayed.

BUNNY nods.

74   INT. BAR

> JOHNNER
> Yeah. You made a bollix of it.

75   INT. PHONE BOX

> GIT
> He doesn't seem to know anything
> about the money.

76   INT. BAR

> JOHNNER
> I don't blame him. I wouldn't tell you
> couple a clowns anything either.

77   INT. PHONE BOX

GIT and BUNNY feel like a couple of clowns.

78   INT. BAR

> JOHNNER
> You still have him . . .

79   INT. PHONE BOX

> GIT
> Yeah, he's in the b . . . He's in the car.

80   INT. BAR

                          JOHNNER
              Frank's bud'll be there again today.
              Bring Frank to him.

81   INT. PHONE BOX

BUNNY nudges GIT.

                            GIT
              Can I speak to Mr. French?

82   INT. BAR

JOHNNER looks at TOM. ANTO sits to one side, watching TV. STEO sits
behind him.

                          JOHNNER
              No, he's gone out.

83   INT. PHONE BOX

GIT looks at BUNNY and shakes his head. BUNNY angrily leaves the
phone box.

84   EXT. COUNTRYSIDE DAY

The car is parked in an uninhabited area. GIT opens the boot. FRANK
GROGAN is very pale and has been sick on himself. He looks up, blinking
at the light. BUNNY leans casually, looking at FRANK.

                          BUNNY
              Morning, Frank.

85   EXT. CAR B DAY

FRANK GROGAN sits in the back. His hands are bound behind him. They
are driving.

                          FRANK
              I can tell yous now. I don't know what
              the hell you're talking about.

                            GIT
              We understand you can't trust us.
              That's why we're gonna take you to
              someone who knows you.

                          FRANK
              It's not that. I honestly don't know what
              you're talking about.

                    BUNNY
          Why do you think we were sent to get
          you?

                    FRANK
          Tom French?

                    GIT
          Yeah.

GIT smokes.

                    FRANK
          Can I have one of them?

GIT gives FRANK a cigarette and lights it for him.

                    FRANK
          I mean, I don't know if this is some
          kind of mix-up or what he's after
          telling you. But there's only one reason
          he'd want to give *me* hassle.

Pause. FRANK smokes.

                    GIT
          What's that?

                    FRANK
          I've been fucking his wife for about
          eighteen months.

                    GIT
          What?

                    FRANK
          That's what I'm telling you.

                    GIT
          So, so what . . . What are we . . . ?

BUNNY pulls in.

                    BUNNY
          Stay there for a sec, Frank.
          (To GIT.) Come here for a minute.

GIT and BUNNY get out.

86   EXT. COUNTRY ROAD DAY

                    BUNNY
          Stop paying attention to that. We gotta
          be very careful here. D'you hear me?
          No matter what this loolah says, it
          doesn't matter. Someone's lying, so
          what? It's none of our business. All we

                    41

gotta do is deliver him and this is over.
I don't care who's fucking who, who's
stroking what. Less we know the
better, believe me. Alright? These are
slippery cunts. Word's no good. Truth's
not important to us. Just the job. (Short
pause.) Okay?

GIT

But what if he's, what if he really *is* . . .

BUNNY

What? What if he is? It doesn't change
the job. (Pause.) If he wants to fuck Tom
French around, that's his business. I'm
not gonna drive him around while he
does it. You have to ignore him. Don't
let him use you. (Short pause.) Come
on. We gotta change the car.

BUNNY sees a town up ahead.

BUNNY

Civilisation. I'll walk in from here, get
fresh wheels. You drive through meet
me on the far side, dump this in a
field.

89   EXT. STREET IN RURAL TOWN DAY

BUNNY is in a phone box.

90   INT. SUBURBAN HOUSE DAY

A little girl (four or five years) answers the phone. Two women are nearby
looking on anxiously.

GIRL

Hello?

91   INT. PHONE BOX

BUNNY

Hello, is that Carol?

92   INT. HOUSE

GIRL

Caroline.

93   INT. PHONE BOX

BUNNY

Hello, love. This is Uncle Bunny.

42

94   INT. HOUSE

                    GIRL (pause)
              Who?

95   INT. PHONE BOX

                         BUNNY
                    Uncle Bunny, Sweetheart. Tell me, is
                    Auntie Teresa there?

96   INT. HOUSE

The two women signal to the child to say 'No'.

                         GIRL
                    Yeah . . .

97   INT. PHONE BOX

                         BUNNY
                    Can I talk to her?

Pause.

                         GIRL
                    No . . .

                         BUNNY
                    No . . . right . . . (Pause.) Will you do
                    something for me, Karen? Will you tell
                    Auntie Teresa that Uncle Bunny loves
                    her?

Pause.

                         GIRL
                    No.

98   INT. CAR B COUNTRYSIDE DAY

GIT has parked the car on the far side of the town. FRANK sighs heavily.
GIT looks at FRANK in the rear-view. He is curious.

                         GIT
                    What were you doing in Cork, Frank?

                         FRANK
                    My family's from Cork. I got a lot of
                    connections with the place. I was
                    meeting French's missus down there
                    for the weekend. Hotel called the
                    Glenwood. She was supposed to come
                    down, Friday evening. She never
                    showed up. And I just, I just knew that

French was on to us. And em . . . my
brother-in-law works with some people
who, you know, would be in the same
business as French. They'd be to Cork,
like he is to Dublin, you know?

                    GIT
And you went to them for help?

                    FRANK
That's why they gave you a hiding

Pause.

                    GIT
How d'you know about that?

                    FRANK
They told me.

Pause.

                    GIT
And there's no money . . . ?

                    FRANK
Fuck it. Son. Do you not think if I had
it, I'd hand it over? I just wanna get
outta this. I'd pay anything to avoid
Tom French. But I don't know anything
about it.

                    GIT
Well that's . . . we gotta go on our
information. Far as we know, there's
money. And you understand, you know,
we got no reason to believe you. And
the thing is, if you're after stealing
twenty-five grand from this deal, we
don't want to have to be the ones who
end up paying for it. Can you
understand that?

                    FRANK
Of course I can. It's all about who you
think you can trust.

GIT sees BUNNY pulling up behind them in a fresh car (Car C).

99   INT. CAR C DAY

BUNNY drives, GIT in the passenger seat, FRANK in the back.

                    FRANK
Where are we going?

44

                         GIT
Gort.

                        FRANK
Where?

                        BUNNY
You excited?

                        FRANK
Will you believe me? If I don't know
this guy?

                        BUNNY
This stage, I'd believe happiness was a
big dick, Frank, you know what I
mean?

GIT laughs.

                         GIT
What does that mean?

                        BUNNY
Don't know. Just said it.

They drive on in silence for a few moments.

                        FRANK
Trussed up like a fucking turkey. Tom
French. He's not gonna do yous any
favours boys. Never did anything for
anybody. There's a ruthlessness in
that man. Even if he liked you, and he
doesn't like anybody. (Pause.) I'm not
like that, boys. Sure I've been
associated with these people. That's
my fault. There's no one I can blame.
I come from a lovely family. Taught me
all sorts a decent things from a very
young age. I have a degree. Did yous
know that? Took it in the evenings.

                        BUNNY
A degree in riding other blokes' wives?

                        FRANK
Ah, now don't say that. Anybody can
fall in love. Don't say that. (Pause.)
Frank Grogan, B.A. See that? Education
can change your name. Change your
life, you let it.

                        BUNNY
Change your mouth into an arsehole.

45

FRANK

That's a real . . . That's a real what Tom
French would say. That's about the
level now. I'll tell you something, and
this is true. I used to work with these
two boys, not much older than you,
son. (Addressing GIT.) And they were
working for me, you know? Lovely
youngfellas, cousins. And one day
I sent one a them down the bookies,
throw a fast bet on for me. Won and all.
But when I went to get it, I found out
the girl had had to fill the docket in for
him. I mean the poor fella. And do you
know what I did? I taught them lads to
read. Tom French, wouldn't occur to
him in a million years, do a thing like
that. I taught them fuckers how to
fucking read, for God's sake. That's
gonna be with me forever.

BUNNY

You gave them boys something to do
while they're banged up for all the
capers you probably got them involved
in, yeah?

FRANK

Aw yeah, big gas. But there's no gift
like giving. You can't beat it. And the
opportunity can come and go, and you
missed it. And it's over.

Short pause.

One thing . . . that you can do . . . as
human *beings* . . . For the sake of
decency . . . and . . . and . . .

BUNNY (annoyed)

What?

FRANK

Few fucking *clothes*, you know?

FRANK looks at GIT and shakes his head.

100   EXT. RURAL TOWN DAY

The car is parked outside a small clothes shop.

101   INT. CAR C DAY

GIT and FRANK sit in the car.

FRANK

How long you been working for
French?

GIT

I don't work for him.

FRANK

What?

GIT

I'm like you, Frank, I don't have a
choice.

FRANK

D'you owe him money?

GIT

Well, that's the big question, isn't it? If
there isn't any, you know?

FRANK

There isn't. (Pause.)

GIT

How'd you get involved with his wife?

FRANK

Ah I know him for years. I was at the
wedding, for fuck's sake. We used to
work together.

GIT

Yeah?

FRANK

Aw yeah. Years ago. Back in the days a
Sonny Mulligan. Mmm. Long time ago
now.

GIT

What happened to him?

FRANK

Sonny? Well that's the thing, isn't it?
Nobody knows.

GIT

Just vanished?

FRANK

Ah you hear different stories. I don't
know. Probably living in the
Caribbean. Millionaire gangster.
Sucking on a cocktail, someone
sucking his cock. He was a true
gentleman that man. A gent.

47

GIT sees BUNNY paying the assistant.

> FRANK
> He's French's boy?

> GIT
> Don't think so.

> FRANK
> D'you not know him?

GIT shakes his head. Pause.

> FRANK
> This fella you're taking me to. What if
> he's got plans to, you know, take care
> of me. In the bad sense. You don't
> mind about that?

> GIT
> I don't think I'd just let something like
> that happen, Frank.

> FRANK
> I'm depending on you, then.

GIT sees BUNNY come out of the shop.

> FRANK
> Do you hear me?

BUNNY gets in.

> FRANK
> I'm only used to the very best.

> BUNNY
> They only stock the best.

They pull away from the kerb.

102   EXT. A LAY-BY DAY

GIT and BUNNY stand leaning on the car, smoking. FRANK is rustling
around in the bushes, changing his clothes. He emerges, holding his
pyjamas in a ball. He is wearing a pair of brown pants easily too small for
him, a blue/green Hawaiian shirt, and a cheap raincoat. FRANK stands
there looking at them accusingly. GIT gapes at the ensemble, but BUNNY
barely reacts, as though nothing is wrong.

> FRANK
> Yous . . . are . . . fucking *bastards*.

GIT suppresses a laugh. FRANK is still in his bare feet.

> FRANK
> Didn't even get me a pair of shoes.

48

                    BUNNY
          Oh I nearly forgot.

BUNNY leans into the car and pulls out a box. He takes out a nice pair
of boots.

                    BUNNY
          What do you think of them?

              FRANK (he likes them)
          They eh, they should do the job.

                    BUNNY
          No these are for me.

                    FRANK
          What am I gonna do?

                    BUNNY
          You can have these ones.

FRANK looks down in dismay at BUNNY's horrible white shoes.

103   INT. CAR C DAY

They are driving as before, FRANK in the back.

                    FRANK
          Women. (Pause.) Are you boys married?
          (Pause.) Sorry, personal question. (Pause.)
          This is a relief in a way, yeah, you know?
          Did you ever make love to a gangster's
          wife? Jesus. You can't really enjoy
          yourself. I mean, I'm not saying . . .
          I mean, she's a smashing little bird,
          French's missus.

                    BUNNY
          I don't really want to hear this, Frank.

              FRANK (conspiratorially)
          Do anything to you. She'd do anything.
          But you know, there you are.
          Consenting adults, perfectly in your
          rights. Relaxing. Having intercourse.

                    BUNNY
          I'm not interested in this, Frank.

                    FRANK
          And human contact, very nice. But
          fuck, all the time, it's like you're
          waiting, just waiting that they're gonna
          get you. Yous have no idea. The fear?
          That's why this is a relief. To be picked
          up by reasonable men. (Pause.) It's . . .

it's like making *love* with the angel
of *death*, fucking, forever sitting at
your . . . your . . .

                    BUNNY
(annoyed, looking in the rear-view mirror)
Would you fucking shut up? You're jab-
bering away there like a . . . fucking . . .
idiot. And the fucking thing is, I mean,
we don't know if . . . (Counting on his
fingers): One, you're bullshitting us.
Two if you're lying, or three, what the
fuck is going on.

GIT gives BUNNY a quizzical sideways glance.

                    BUNNY
So give it a fucking rest, alright?

                    FRANK
Cool your jets, I'm just talking.

                    BUNNY
That's all you fucking do is talk.

GIT sees something up ahead.

                    GIT
Bunny . . .

                    BUNNY
And it's like I'm this close to putting
you back in the fucking boot. And you
can fucking . . .

                    GIT
Bunny . . .

                    BUNNY
. . . Stay there . . .

                    GIT
Bunny, look.

Up ahead there is a crash. A GUARD is directing traffic around it. BUNNY
is now too close to turn back.

                    BUNNY
Undo his hands, quick.

FRANK turns to allow GIT to untie him, looking over his shoulder. GIT
looks at FRANK carefully, letting him see his hand on his pistol.

                    GIT
Don't let us down here, Frank.

FRANK

You know it.

The GUARD signals for them to stop, walks to the car. BUNNY rolls down the window.

GUARD

Give us a minute, men. Nothing
serious.

The GUARD straightens up, watches the road being cleared. GIT glances down, sees BUNNY move his hand inside his jacket. GIT looks around at FRANK, who gives him a little smile. The GUARD ambles back to them.

GUARD

Are yous local?

BUNNY

No, just passing through. Couple a
days off.

GUARD

Well for yous. You know your tax is two
months out?

BUNNY

I know, Guard. It's a company car, I've
been at them for weeks.

GUARD

You'd want to get it sorted out. Save
yourself the hassle.

FRANK
(to GIT and BUNNY's horror)
Yeah, they were the same with me last
year. I ended up paying it myself. It
was easier in the end, get them to
reimburse you.

BUNNY

Eh, yeah, I'll, I'll probably do that.

GUARD

Mm. Where are yous headed?

BUNNY

Em . . . eh, his auntie. (Indicates GIT.)
Where is it, Mick?

Pause.

GIT

Ennis.

GUARD (nods)
You'll be there in about three quarters
of an hour.

51

                         FRANK
            Not the way he drives, Guard.

                         GUARD
            Is that right, yeah? You've a bit of Cork.

                         FRANK
            Family down there.

                         GUARD
            You can hear it.

GIT doesn't know what to do. BUNNY seethes.

                         FRANK
            Where you from yourself?

                         GUARD
            Originally from Clare, not too far from
            Ennis, actually. Would I know your
            relations?

                          GIT
            She only moved there last year.

                         GUARD
            Oh right.

Pause.

                         BUNNY
            I think we're okay now.

The GUARD turns the road is clear.

                         GUARD
            Okay, well, good luck, boys.

                         BUNNY
            Thanks, Guard, thanks very much.

                         FRANK
            All the best.

They drive on.

                         FRANK
            Now! How was that, ha? Who's on
            who's side now?

No one says anything, BUNNY checks the road. He pulls into a secluded
place.

                         FRANK
            What are you doing?

BUNNY gets out and opens the boot.

                    BUNNY
        Come on.

                    FRANK
        What? And me after being brilliant
        with the guard and everything?

104   INT. CAR C DAY

It's now just GIT and BUNNY driving.

                    GIT
        What if he doesn't know this bloke?

                    BUNNY
        Then he might be telling the truth, you
        know? But, I mean, I wouldn't put it
        past this geebag to let *on* he doesn't
        know him. Get outta paying what he
        owes. You know that way? (Pause.)
        I don't trust him, Git.

Pause.

                    GIT
        This job. Clear your debts with French?

                    BUNNY
        You must be joking, sometimes feels
        like I'm gonna be beholden to that
        fucker the rest a my days.

                    GIT
        Would you not just try and go
        somewhere, away from him?

                    BUNNY
        Can't just drop things, you know? In
        any case, not down to just me. (Short
        pause.) The missus and all, you know?
        (Pause.) It's never that easy.

        ┌─────────────────────────────────────┐
        │   'Back on the bog. A dirty deal,   │
        │   and then a cleaner deal.'   │
        │   │
        └─────────────────────────────────────┘

105   EXT. BOGLAND EVENING.

The car sits back where they were yesterday. The garage. The caravan.
And now a car that wasn't there before.

106   INT. CAR C EVENING

GIT and BUNNY.

> BUNNY
> Fucking place . . . I'm not going across
> that bog again. You bring him over and
> don't fall into any fucking holes.

Pause.

> GIT
> I'm gonna check it out.

GIT gets out.

> BUNNY
> What? Ah for fuck's sake.

107   EXT. BOG DAY

GIT goes across to the garage.

108   EXT. GARAGE DAY

GIT approaches.

> GIT
> Hello?

A MAN steps out of the garage.

> MAN
> Howya. You with Frank?

> GIT
> Yeah, you know him, yeah?

> MAN
> Aw yeah. Frank, yeah. I'll take it from
> here.

Pause.

> GIT
> Okay. I'll get him.

109   EXT. BOG DAY

GIT comes back to the car.

> GIT
> Look. If there's any trouble . . .

> BUNNY
> What trouble? Bring him over. Dump
> him, come back, we go home.

Pause.

                    BUNNY
What . . . ?

                    GIT
I sorta said . . . I wouldn't leave him
if . . .

                    BUNNY
What did I tell you? What did I say?

                    GIT
I know . . .

                    BUNNY
These shits'll do anything to get their
way. Now you take that bastard over
there, cash on delivery. You're back
here two minutes or I'm gone, 'cause
you love him so much, you're welcome
to him. Now, get out and do it.

Pause.

                    GIT
Just 'do it'. That's all there is for you?

                    BUNNY
That's all there is, Chicolito. Because
and I'll tell you why. One, there's no
room, for anything else. Two. You gotta
leave, and quite fucking simply, you
gotta leave room for yourself. And
three . . .

                    GIT
Stop it Bunny. (Short pause.) You're the
same as him. It's all mouth. (Short
pause.) What if that was you in the
boot? (Short pause.)

                    BUNNY
I don't *care*. Do you see?

Pause.

                    GIT
No. I don't.

GIT goes to the boot and opens it.

                    FRANK
Where is he?

                    GIT
We have to go across here.

                    55

GIT helps FRANK out of the boot. FRANK clings to him a little. GIT leads him onto the bog and they walk.

> FRANK
> I've never been here before. I don't know this place, is what I'm saying! (Pause.) Please don't make me go in there.

> GIT
> I'm not gonna leave you. We'll see who's here.

> FRANK
> You promise me?

> GIT
> I won't leave you in the shit.

110   EXT. GARAGE AND CARAVAN

The door to the garage is open. As they approach, GIT sees a MAN arranging a tarpaulin sheet on the floor.

> GIT
> Hello?

The MAN comes out, pulling the door behind him.

> GIT
> Howya.

> MAN
> Alright?

> FRANK
> I don't know him. Git, I . . . I don't know him.

> GIT
> Do you know Frank?

> MAN
> *I* don't. No. The fella was supposed to be here yesterday, couldn't come today.

> FRANK
> What's his name?

> MAN
> I don't know.

> GIT
> 'Cause you see, I'm supposed to hand Frank over to a friendly face.

Pause.

MAN
You don't like my face?

GIT
What? It's just I'm telling you what . . .
you know, what I'm supposed to do.

MAN
You go on, now, let me take care of
him.

FRANK (to GIT)
I'll be on your conscience forever if you
leave me here.

MAN
There's nothing to worry about. But
you hang around, you know, you're
gonna give me a problem here.

GIT
Well, I need some sort of . . .

The MAN produces a gun.

MAN
Makes no odds to me. Both of you in.

FRANK (to GIT)
I said this! Where's your . . . ?

FRANK gestures to GIT to take out his gun. GIT closes his eyes in dismay.

MAN
Yeah. I think I'd like to see that as well.
Slowly . . .

FRANK
Sorry.

GIT slowly takes his gun out.

MAN
Throw it over there.

GIT throws the gun to one side.

MAN
Inside.

111   INT. RUNDOWN GARAGE DAY

They come in. It is dusty, disused.

MAN
Kneel down on that tarp.

57

                         FRANK
              There's no need for this.

                         MAN
              Just do it.

They kneel. The MAN points the gun at FRANK's head.

                         FRANK
              Whatever you're getting, how much are
              you getting? Five? Ten? Twenty? I'll
              give you fifty.

The MAN hesitates.

                         FRANK
              I'll give you fifty grand to let me walk
              away from this. We can go to my bank
              in the morning.

Pause. The MAN considers.

                         MAN (to GIT)
              What'll you give me?

                         GIT
              I don't have anything.

                         FRANK
              Fuck him! This is you and me. Forget
              about him. He's nothing to do with any
              deal that you and I make.

Pause.

                         MAN
              Okay.

He levels his gun at GIT.

                         BUNNY
              There had better be a very fucking
              good explanation for this.

BUNNY is leaning around the doorway, his pistol trained on the MAN. Very
little of himself exposed.

                         FRANK
              Bunny! Thank God! Talk some sense
              into this maniac.

                         BUNNY
              Drop it.

The MAN drops his gun.

                         BUNNY
              Git, get up and come on.

                    FRANK
What about me?

                    BUNNY
You're not my problem. The two a you
go to your bank. See you round.

                    FRANK
I was just buying time! I knew you
were gonna come through for us.
Great! You know?

          BUNNY (short pause)
Fuck you.

                    FRANK
Think about it. I buy my way outta this
and I'm still at large . . . You think Tom
French is gonna be happy with your
work?

                    BUNNY
Not our fault. We're not letting you go.
(Indicates MAN.) Charles Bronson is.

                    FRANK
I can cut us all a deal. Get everybody
what they want. All I need is a phone.

                    BUNNY
Face it, Frank. You blew it.

                    FRANK
I can get you a good thing here. Get
French off your back for good, and
I mean that.

                    BUNNY
What, 'cause you're fucking his wife?
I don't think so.

                    FRANK
There's some money . . . that we have
to sort out.

                    BUNNY
Oh really? I wouldna thought that.

                    FRANK
I know, I know. Okay, big joke. But this
is the truth, I can sort us out.

                    GIT
Bunny, em, can I talk to you for a sec.

GIT goes to BUNNY. BUNNY keeps his gun trained on the MAN and
FRANK.

                    59

                    GIT (quietly)
          There's two things here. He pays his
          way outta whatever this is. He's right,
          we'll get the fucking blame. All
          everybody's been doing is lying to us.
          But we hang on to him. Do this on our
          terms. We can walk away. 'Cause
          French wants this bad. (Pause.) I say
          let's stop fucking around and *use* this
          bastard.

Pause.

                    BUNNY (to FRANK)
          Who do you wanna ring?

                    FRANK
          Who do you think?

                    MAN
          That would help me actually. If I could
          get someone on my behalf that this
          isn't my fault. I have a mobile.

                    BUNNY
          I don't fucking believe this.

                    MAN
          It's in my car.

112   EXT. GARAGE DAY

GIT, FRANK, the MAN and BUNNY come out of the garage and go to
the MAN'S car.

                    BUNNY
          How did you get your car in here?

                    MAN
          What do you mean?

                    BUNNY
          We're parked on the other side of the
          bog.

                    MAN
          Why are you on the back road?

                    BUNNY
          Yeah, well it's more scenic, isn't it?
          Give him the keys.

The MAN hands GIT the keys. GIT opens the car and takes the phone.

                    BUNNY
          Put him in first class.

GIT opens the boot. It is completely lined with black plastic bags.

> GIT

Get in.

113   INT. CAR C DAY

The light is fading. BUNNY, GIT and FRANK. GIT holds the mobile phone on his lap.

> FRANK
> I had . . . a plate. A plate for printing
> one side of a twenty dollar note. I got it
> dead cheap, years ago, I mean what
> use are one-sided forgeries? And since
> then, I been tryna find if anyone could
> get me the other side. To do the . . . the
> backs. And I haven't been able to,
> right? But then, all of a sud, Tom
> French gets the other side. Don't ask
> me where, I don't know. Word goes out.
> 'Who's got the rest of this, who's got
> the other half?' I go way back with
> French, we used to work together, and
> I offer . . .

> BUNNY
> This was with Sonny Mulligan?

> FRANK
> Ah years ago. This has nothing to do
> with Sonny. Me and Tom French have
> been more or less out of touch since
> Sonny went. We fell out over . . . a
> certain ladyfriend. But, I rang him up,
> let bygones be bygones, and I offered
> to buy his side of the . . . the other one,
> the other plate. But . . . French is
> having none of it, too greedy, wants
> them both, and he'll buy *my* one off
> me! For five grand! I ask you! So I go
> 'Bollix, no way . . . ' 'Cause now that
> we know the other one at least exists,
> it's worth a lot more than that. But at
> the same time, without the other one
> my one is useless. So it's like 'I've arsed
> around with this long enough, I'll sell
> it.' But not for any five grand. No
> problem finding a higher bidder. This
> bloke from England, *ten* grand, thank
> you very much. But then, just before
> I'm about to meet this bloke, Tom
> French rings me again. Says he's found
> a buyer for both plates. (Pause.) And

he's been offered a hundred grand.
Says he can give me twenty-five up
front as a goodwill . . . fucking . . .
gesture. And his wife will bring it
down. In return for the plate. I'm doing
well. The worst I can get is twenty-five,
even if he thinks he's ripping me off.
So I'm there all ready to do the deal in
the Glenwood with his missus. She
never shows! Next thing I know, yous
are pulling me out of the scratcher, and
people are trying to kill me. And that's
all I know.

                    BUNNY
Wait a minute, wait a minute. What?

Pause.

                    FRANK
What do you mean, 'What?'

                    BUNNY
What do you think I mean? I mean,
'What?'

Pause.

                    FRANK
What? You mean 'The whole *thing*'
what?

BUNNY looks at GIT as though FRANK is unbelievably thick.

                    BUNNY
It's a very simple question. What are
you . . . ? . . . What did you have, that
. . . time?

FRANK looks at GIT. Pause.

                    BUNNY
You fucking dawbrain.

114   EXT. COUNTRY ROAD EVENING

The car is parked.

115   INT. PARKED CAR C EVENING

GIT holds the phone.

                    GIT
Mr. French, please. (Short pause.) Git.

                              TOM
             Yes.

                              GIT
             Frank's pal wanted to kill him.

Pause.

                              TOM
             You still got him?

                              GIT
             Yeah.

                              TOM
             What do you want to do?

                              GIT
             Make a deal, where no one gets killed,
             if that's okay by you.

Pause.

                              TOM
             Ask Frank if he wants to do what
             Sonny mighta wanted.

                   GIT (to FRANK)
             He wants to know if you want to do
             what Sonny mighta wanted?

                             FRANK
             When?

                   GIT (to TOM)
             When?

                              TOM
             In the morning. He'll know where to
             go. I'll be alone.

                              GIT
             What about Anto?

                              TOM
             He'll be tucked up with his girlfriend
             by midnight.

        TOM hangs up.

                              63

> 'Some TV. Some R&R.
> A discourse on aesthetics.
> A terrible secret. Some dancing
> and some sexual intercourse.'

116   EXT. HOTEL NIGHT

A modern hotel in the countryside, a bit of evening trade going into an adjoining night-club.

117   INT. HOTEL LOBBY NIGHT

GIT, BUNNY and FRANK are in a quiet hotel lobby. GIT checks them in while BUNNY and FRANK sit on the furniture. A receptionist attends to GIT. She hands him a form.

> RECEPTIONIST
> How will you be paying, Mr. Guinness?

> GIT
> Cash.

118   INT. HOTEL ROOM NIGHT

GIT and BUNNY are tying FRANK to a bed, running the ropes underneath.

> FRANK
> Jesus, boys. I woulda thought that at
> this stage, this was getting a bit
> unnecessary.

> BUNNY
> We *really* need a little . . . break from
> you, Frank. And this way you can kip!

BUNNY props FRANK's head up with pillows. Places the TV remote in his hand.

> BUNNY
> Watch the box. Whatever.

GIT and BUNNY begin to leave.

> FRANK
> What are yous doing?

> BUNNY
> Shame to waste the facilities.

> FRANK
> What if I need the toilet?

> BUNNY
> Shoulda gone before we came out.

GIT and BUNNY leave. FRANK lies still for a moment. He manages to manipulate the remote control. The TV comes on. It is a programme about gardening. FRANK tries to change the channel. The remote falls off the bed. FRANK is left facing it.

> FRANK
> Oh my God . . .

119   INT. SWIMMING POOL NIGHT

GIT and BUNNY have the pool to themselves. They jump in. Swim around, very tranquil.

120   INT. BAR NIGHT

There is a bit of a buzz in the bar. GIT and BUNNY sit drinking.

> GIT
> First pint in eight months.

> BUNNY
> You lucky bastard. That's gonna taste gorgeous. (Irritated.) Fuck! It's like I got his mouth living in my ear. I can . . . still hear him. I swear to God, it's like he's here, 'I taught my dog how to read porno mags . . . ' All this. Fuck me.

Pause. GIT smiles.

> BUNNY
> What do you think about this? Tomorrow.

> GIT
> You asking me?

> BUNNY
> Don't get smart, come on.

> GIT (short pause)
> Chance find out what . . . Only chance get outta this. I mean what the *fuck* are we into here?

> BUNNY
> What are we into?

> GIT
> Yeah.

> BUNNY
> We are up to our bollocks in some real old time gangster fucking . . . row. 'I'm riding your wife.' 'You're wearing my wig.' 'I had Sonny Mulligan's dick up my arse two nights on the trot in 1971.'

GIT laughs.

> **BUNNY**
> D'you know what I mean?

> **GIT**
> Mmm.

> **BUNNY**
> Saps.

> **GIT**
> D'you want another one?

> **BUNNY**
> Another *one*?

> **GIT** (gets BARMAID's attention)
> Could I eh . . . ? Thanks.

Pause.

BUNNY sees that the news is on the TV.

> **BUNNY** (to BARMAID)
> Sorry, could you turn that up please?

The sound comes up.

> **NEWSREADER**
> And the headlines again. Gardai are
> investigating reports of a shooting at a
> house outside Cork city early this
> morning. And in what is believed to be
> an unrelated incident a Dublin
> businessman was discovered in the
> boot of his car, near Gort. Cash and a
> mobile phone were stolen. And that's
> all from me for this evening. The next
> news will be the late headlines at a
> quarter past eleven. Until then, good
> evening.

> **GIT**
> Cash?

> **BUNNY**
> Cheeky bollox.

A man further down the bar was also watching the news.

> **MAN**
> The scumbags are taking over now. It's
> getting vicious.

> **BUNNY**
> Doesn't look like anybody got hurt.

MAN

They're fucking scum.

BUNNY

Who's fucking scum?

GIT

Cool it. What are you doing?

BUNNY calms down.

BUNNY

Who's this mate a yours? Good mate?

GIT

Anto, yeah. Best friends since we were
six. He's eh you know, as well, like,
he's going out with this bird I used to
be with.

BUNNY

Yeah? That when you were inside?

GIT

Yeah. You know . . .

BUNNY

That's tough.

GIT

Yeah, just wanna get this over with.
Get away you know?

BUNNY

Yeah?

The drinks arrive.

BUNNY

Where would you go?

GIT

Dunno. States? Don't care.

BUNNY

The States is brilliant.

GIT

You been there?

BUNNY

Yeah. Nah, I mean just, on the telly and
that . . .

GIT

Fucking chancer . . .

67

Pause. They drink. GIT looks around. He sees a phone. Someone is using it.

>   GIT
> See you in a minute.

GIT gets up.

121   INT. HOTEL LOBBY NIGHT

GIT comes out of the bar and goes to a phone. He puts in a handful of change.

>   GIT
> Hello, could I speak to Sabrina please?
> Thanks.

>   SABRINA
> Hello?

>   GIT
> Hiya, it's Git.

>   SABRINA
> Where are you?

>   GIT
> We'll be back tomorrow.

>   SABRINA
> Is Anto there?

>   GIT
> He's having a swim.

>   SABRINA
> Very nice.

>   GIT
> How are things?

>   SABRINA
> Why do you keep ringing me?

>   GIT
> What?

>   SABRINA
> You ring me every day. It's not good,
> you know?

Pause.

>   GIT
> Just. I'm . . . I mightn't be around later
> on. And. I'm tryna get used to this.

Pause.

                    SABRINA
          These things happen.

                    GIT
          Yeah.

                    SABRINA
          You're gonna have to forget about it
          now.

Pause.

                    GIT
          You shouldn't have done it, though.

                    SABRINA
          I don't go out with criminals.

                    GIT
          I don't blame you.

                    SABRINA
          And I'm telling you. If you get Anto
          into trouble I'll never talk to you again.
          (Pause.) I have to go.

                    GIT
          Take care.

She hangs up. GIT stands there for a moment.

122   INT. BAR NIGHT

BUNNY is using the phone. All he hears is a ring. No answer. He sees GIT
come back in. He hangs up.

123   INT. BUNNY'S HOUSE NIGHT

Phone rings out.

124   INT. BAR NIGHT

BUNNY and GIT are back at the bar. It's busier.

                    BUNNY
          I'm not . . . educated like . . . Fucko up
          there. But I have this theory about the
          ladies. A good-looking bird. Goes
          around the place all her life, cunts
          looking at her, coming on to her, tryna
          fuck her. Pretty soon she's gonna have
          the opinion that life is full of romance.
          At work, in the pub, life is . . . basically

                    69

full of romantic fucking . . . you know,
sex. That's the way . . .

                    GIT
Yeah . . .

                    BUNNY
That's the way she sees life . . . Like
that. *Ugly* bird, goes through life more
balanced. No chance of a ride. Forgets
about it. Proper outlook. 'I'm not gonna
go around treating everybody like I'm
some bitch, doesn't have to make an
effort . . . because my . . . tits give me a
licence to . . . whatever.' You know?

                    GIT
And what's the . . .

                    BUNNY
Well, you know . . . I'm still working on
the theory. But it's a thing about,
maybe ugly birds are better.

Pause.

                    GIT
How long you been married?

Pause.

                    BUNNY
Twelve years.

Pause.

                    BUNNY
Yeah. You know . . . Tryna . . . She's
staying with her sister. For a little
while. You know . . . It's that fucking
thing, Git, armed robbery. Did six and
a half years. You know, you can't, you
lose . . . you lose a lot of, em . . .
(Pause.)

There was a . . . a man, a man I shared
a cell with, for two, three months. And
what went on. It wasn't . . . full . . .
I'm being frank with you here. Not
that Frank, not Frank upstairs, Frank.
(Little laugh.) I'm not a queer, but Tom
French . . . says he'll tell . . . My wife
doesn't know. And that'd tear it. That'd
fuck it up. If she knew. So . . . Here
I am. (Pause.) I haven't told anyone
else, so . . .

70

                              GIT
                    Don't worry about it.

                             BUNNY
                    Dunno. Sometimes feels like that cunt
                    is all over me. All over the fucking
                    place.

Pause. They drink. BUNNY notices GIT looking at two women.

                             BUNNY
                    Been a while?

                              GIT
                    I'm only out two days, man. I'd have
                    that arse ridden off that quicker than
                    you could get your glasses off for a
                    dig.

                             BUNNY
                    Yeah?

BUNNY takes his drink and gets up.

                              GIT
                    Wait. What are you doing?

                             BUNNY
                    What do you think?

BUNNY goes over to the women.

                              GIT
                    Bunny!

125   INT. HOTEL ROOM NIGHT

       FRANK lies tied to the bed, still looking at the telly. An Open University
       programme is now on. It is black and white, made in the seventies,
       algebra.

126   INT. HOTEL NIGHT-CLUB NIGHT

       GIT and BUNNY are bopping with the women. One of them puts her arms
       around GIT. BUNNY and his girlfriend are dancing very sexily. GIT and
       BUNNY exchange grins.

127   INT. BAR DISCO

       GIT and his GIRLFRIEND are at the bar.

       Pause.

                           GIRLFRIEND
                    Do you ever talk?

                               71

Yeah.

Pause. They laugh.

GIRLFRIEND
What do you say?

GIT
I say things like 'Are we going to the
shops?' That type of thing.

They laugh.

GIRLFRIEND
You're afraid I'm going to find
something out.

GIT
Yeah?

GIRLFRIEND
And I'm going to have something on
you. Isn't that it? (Pause.) Because you
know, I've already got something.

GIT
Yeah? What have you got?

The GIRLFRIEND sticks her thumb up.

GIRLFRIEND
Squeeze my thumb as hard as you can.

Pause. GIT smiles and grabs her thumb.

GIRLFRIEND
As hard as you can. Okay. Now
squeeze it with the other hand.

GIT does so.

GIRLFRIEND
Now.

GIT
What . . .

GIRLFRIEND
I know something about you.

GIT
What . . .

GIRLFRIEND
I know what hand you wank with.
That's all life's about.

128   INT. TOILETS NIGHT

GIT and BUNNY are having a piss. We still hear music from the disco.

> GIT
> Bunny, man. She's gone to get a room.

> BUNNY
> You dirty little bastard.

> GIT
> How would that be, if I saw you in the
> morning? You know, with Frank and
> that?

> BUNNY
> Leave Frank to me.

> GIT
> You're a star.

> BUNNY
> Jesus Christ! You've got a hard-on now!

> GIT
> Don't look at it!

> BUNNY
> You're very big for a lad your age . . .

> GIT
> Leave me alone. Go up to Frank.

GIT leaves.

> BUNNY
> Don't hurt the poor girl!

129   INT. CORRIDOR NIGHT

BUNNY sneaks down a hotel corridor, and looks around a corner. He sees
GIT and his GIRLFRIEND go into a room. He goes to the door and listens.

130   INT. HOTEL ROOM

GIT and his GIRLFRIEND are kissing and feeling each other. GIT puts his
hands up her top. They laugh. GIT stops. As though he has heard
something. He senses BUNNY.

> GIRLFRIEND
> What's wrong?

> GIT
> Sorry. Hold on a sec.

GIT goes to the door and looks out into the corridor. BUNNY is not outside
the door. He is, however, walking towards the room. GIT frowns.

BUNNY
Ah! There you are. Night now.

> 'Then do you agree with me
> that on average a woman
> is in her prime for twenty years,
> and a man for thirty?'
>
> Plato, *The Republic*

131   EXT. HOTEL EARLY MORNING

It's very quiet. Bit of birdsong, no traffic.

132   INT. A HOTEL ROOM EARLY MORNING (before dawn)

GIT and his girlfriend are still making love. They stop and look at each other.

GIRL
You're very good.

GIT
Yeah?

GIRL
You know you are.

GIT
How would I know?

GIRL
Does your girlfriend not tell you?

GIT
No girlfriend.

GIRL
No . . . ?

GIT
That's why I need the practice.

GIRL (shakes her head)
It's in your approach. (Pause.) And you're very big.

GIT
Does that count?

74

The GIRL nods.

                    GIRL
        Does for me.

                    GIT
        I haven't . . . been with anyone for a
        while.

                    GIRL
        Saving it for someone special?

She raises her eyebrows as if to say 'Like me?'

                    GIT
        Em. I should . . . 'cause, we're, em.
        I was in prison. But you know I'm
        saying immediately, I'm not . . . You're
        safe with me.

                    GIRL
        You're reformed, yeah?

                    GIT
        Oh ye . . . I was reformed before I went
        into the fucking place.

                    GIRL
        What did you do?

                    GIT
        Ah. It was . . . stupid. I . . . took me
        dad out for a few drinks one night,
        last year. And he was. All his life,
        emphysema, couldn't work or that.
        Loved his drink. But a terrible messy
        fucking drinker. And I took him out.
        Lashed a few scoops back, and I was
        walking home with him. And we saw
        these cun . . . these fellas ram, ram-
        raid a shop. A, an electrical shop.
        Alarms going. The works. They
        grabbed hi-fis and all this. Into their
        car and off they went. And this fucking
        eejit beside me, says he wants a video.
        Walks into the shop. And picks one up.
        And I was trying to get him to leave it
        down, and the guards came and
        snared us by the cacks. Down the cop
        shop, the whole bit. They put the video
        in a bag as evidence and everything.
        And eh . . . I said I'd done it.

                    GIRL
        Why?

75

GIT

I was looking at the oldfella. He didn't
even know what the fuck was going
on. Singing rebel songs at the guards
and all this. He was . . . my dad you
know. He couldna . . . he was too weak.
So I said it was me. Went up before
this bollocks of a judge. And I'd been
in a little bit of trouble years and years
before. Messing only, like. Sent me
down for eight months. And then two
weeks later I got word. The old lad
kicked it anyway. Heart. Waste of
fucking time. And, I was getting a loan
for my . . . girlfriend. She was gonna
go to her . . . sister's wedding. In
Australia. And you know, I couldn't . . .
get the loan then. The . . . Credit
Union. So . . . And that's how I lost my
girlfriend.

GIRL

Did you not tell her the truth?

GIT

Nah . . . Tsss. Trying to blame a poor
dead fella. Sure that's worse. I made
the commitment. Head down. And now
I'm out.

GIRL
(putting her hand under the covers)
Yeah. You're at large.

133   INT. ANOTHER HOTEL ROOM EARLY MORNING (before dawn)

BUNNY wakes up with a massive fart. He is beside his girlfriend. He lifts
the sheet and has a sneaky look at her body. Then he sees something. Her
teeth are in a glass of water on the bedside locker. He gets up. Bad
hangover. Sees the time.

BUNNY (whispers)
Shit!

134   INT. HOTEL CORRIDOR MORNING. (before dawn)

BUNNY knocks on a door.

BUNNY
Git. Git.

135   INT. HOTEL ROOM MORNING (before dawn)

This is the room where FRANK was tied. The ropes are on the floor.
FRANK is gone. GIT and BUNNY stand in silence.

> GIT
> What were you doing?

> BUNNY
> Same as you.

> GIT
> Fuck it. Come on.

136   INT. HALLWAY MORNING (before dawn)

GIT and BUNNY are quickly going down the hall, sometimes breaking into
a little trot.

137   INT. LOBBY MORNING (before dawn)

As GIT and BUNNY go through the lobby, the RECEPTIONIST sees them.

> RECEPTIONIST
> Excuse me. Excuse me.

> BUNNY
> What . . . sorry. We're in a hurry.

> RECEPTIONIST
> Will you settle this bill please?

> GIT
> Paid in advance.

> RECEPTIONIST
> This is phone calls.

GIT grabs BUNNY, stopping him.

> GIT
> Sorry?

> RECEPTIONIST
> There's three calls made from your
> room.

> BUNNY
> That fucking motormouth fucking . . .
> We're not paying for his calls. I'm not
> paying.

> GIT
> How much is it?

> RECEPTIONIST (hands GIT a bill)
> Two eighty.

                              BUNNY
               Cheap fucking . . .

                               GIT
               Can I query this? Can I see the
               numbers I'm supposed to have . . .
               have called here?

                          RECEPTIONIST
               Of course . . .

                              BUNNY
               Come on quick. You're not gonna
               pay it . . . ?

BUNNY takes money from his pocket. Puts it on the desk.

                               GIT
               I just wanna check the numbers first.

                              BUNNY
               We don't have time for this.

                               GIT
               Be one sec . . .

                          RECEPTIONIST
               Alright. Two local calls and one . . . it's
               a Cork number.

                              BUNNY
               He's in Cork. Come on.

                               GIT
               D'you recognise the local numbers?

                          RECEPTIONIST
               This is a local taxi company.

                              BUNNY
               Come on . . .

                          RECEPTIONIST
               And this is . . . I think. That's the Slieve
               Na Vogue. It's a hotel about five miles
               away, towards Mullingar.

                              BUNNY
               I'm gonna kill him.

138   INT. CAR C MORNING (before dawn)

GIT and BUNNY drive very fast. While their conversation goes on, they
overtake dangerously.

                              BUNNY
         So?

                               78

GIT

So, yeah?

BUNNY

You know . . .

GIT

You wannna talk about that *now*?
(Pause.)

BUNNY

Well, you know, I'm chasing this loser.
And we lost him 'cause a being stuck
into them tarts. Might be they're the
only good thing could come outta this
whole marvellous few days. And I'm
that annoyed now, that that's what I
wanna . . . dwell upon rather than . . .
any . . . So tell me.

GIT

What . . . ?

BUNNY

She had big tits, your one.

GIT

Yeah. But I don't really like big tits.

BUNNY

Do you not? Two big . . . chewy . . .
melons.

GIT

Chewy *what*?

BUNNY

Well whatever. You're an ass man. I
can respect that. But, what I want is
the fruit, not the pips. But that's me.

Pause. GIT shakes his head in wonder. Laughs.

BUNNY

How old do you reckon they were?

GIT

How old? I don't know. Same age as
me? Bit older maybe?

BUNNY

Bit older, yeah?

GIT

I don't know, maybe.

BUNNY

A *bit* older, Yeah?

'The value of an education.
A shoot-out and a chase
with more shooting.'

139   EXT. SLIEVE NA VOGUE HOTEL EARLY MORNING

GIT and BUNNY pull into the carpark.

140   INT. LOBBY EARLY MORNING

GIT and BUNNY go to the reception. There is no receptionist. GIT looks
through the registration. BUNNY looks around.

>   BUNNY
>   Is he there?

>   GIT
>   Don't think so.

>   BUNNY
>   Show.

We see a close-up of the register. BUNNY runs his finger down. There is
no 'Frank Grogan'. BUNNY runs past a name and then goes back to it.
'Pat Shanks, BA.'

>   BUNNY
>   Pat Shanks . . . B.A. . . .

141   INT. HOTEL CORRIDOR EARLY MORNING

GIT and BUNNY are at a door. GIT listens at it and shrugs at BUNNY.
BUNNY motions GIT out of the way, and draws his pistol. He takes a step
back and kicks the door in.

142   INT. FRANK'S HOTEL ROOM EARLY MORNING

The bathroom is just inside the door. FRANK is having a bath. He splashes
into life as BUNNY comes straight in, followed by GIT. BUNNY gets into
the bath with FRANK, sitting on him. He puts the barrel of his pistol into
FRANK'S mouth.

>   BUNNY
>   Now, you motormouth fucking eejit,
>   d'you want to tell me all about your
>   BA. BA? Yeah? Well, I'm Professor F.
>   Fucking Kelly and I'm here to give
>   you a lecture in gunshot wounds to
>   the face you sneaky little fucking . . .
>   in-the-bath-fella (Pause, low.) I'm that

close to just getting rid of you . . .
D'you know what I mean? Now get up
and put your clothes on you tubby little
no dick lying little fucker, come on.

BUNNY lifts FRANK up out of the bath.

143   INT. HOTEL ROOM EARLY MORNING.

GIT stands looking out the window at the carpark. Behind him BUNNY
brings FRANK into the room.

                    FRANK
          Howya Git.

                    BUNNY
          Don't fucking mind him, come on. Get
          dressed.

                    FRANK
          Give us a towel.

                    BUNNY
          Fuck that, come on, put your clothes
          on, you're making me sick. Come on.

GIT sees a van pull into the carpark. Men get out. GIT recognises them as
the men from Cork.

                    GIT
          They're here.

144   INT. HOTEL CORRIDOR EARLY MORNING

GIT and BUNNY bring FRANK out of the room. They both have their pistols
drawn. They lead him down the corridor. They get to a corner. BUNNY has
a quick look. Two of the CORK MEN are coming towards them. BUNNY
comes back pushing GIT and FRANK. BUNNY keeps his gun to FRANK's
head as they run down the corridor. They get out of sight just as the
CORK MEN come round the corner.

145   INT. STAIRWELL EARLY MORNING

GIT comes down the stairs to a landing, checks, and signals back up to
BUNNY. BUNNY holds his pistol to FRANK's head bringing him down.

146   INT. HOTEL LOBBY EARLY MORNING

GIT, BUNNY and FRANK come into the lobby. GIT looks around a corner.
Two CORK MEN stand at the main entrance. GIT comes back, signals
to BUNNY.

147 INT. RESTAURANT EARLY MORNING

Hotel patrons are eating their breakfast. BUNNY pushes FRANK into the room, gun to his head. GIT follows. Waiters and diners are startled.

> BUNNY
> Table for three please. Near the
> window.

GIT opens an emergency exit.

148 EXT. HOTEL EARLY MORNING

GIT, BUNNY and FRANK come round the side of the hotel into the carpark. They get to their car. BUNNY opens the boot. GIT watches the hotel.

> BUNNY
> Come on, Frank, you know the drill.

BUNNY helps FRANK climb into the boot.

> BUNNY
> I hope you're sickened.

BUNNY slams the boot.

> BUNNY
> Come on . . .

GIT sees two of the CORK MEN looking at them from the hotel. BUNNY is getting into the car.

> GIT
> Bunny . . .

BUNNY looks.

> BUNNY
> Get in.

The CORK MEN begin to come towards them, putting hands in their jackets. GIT opens his door. BUNNY starts the car.

> BUNNY
> Put something over their heads.

> GIT
> What?

BUNNY begins to reverse.

> BUNNY
> Have you got your gun?

> GIT
> Yeah.

                    BUNNY
         Shoot it.

                     GIT
         What?

                    BUNNY
         Shoot! Just fire it!

GIT sees one of the men take a pistol from his jacket. Short pause. GIT
takes his pistol and levels it. The CORK MEN duck behind cars. GIT
shoots, not really aiming at anything. He shoots five times jogging along
with the car. He gets in. They speed away.

149   INT. CAR C EARLY MORNING.

GIT and BUNNY are driving away from the hotel.

                    BUNNY
         They're gonna come, you out?

                     GIT
         What?

                    BUNNY
         You out? Outta ammo?

                     GIT
         Yeah.

                    BUNNY
         Come on. Take this.

BUNNY takes his pistol, handing it to GIT.

                     GIT
         Aw, Jesus, Bunny. Come on. I can't be
         doing this.

                    BUNNY
         It's nothing. Just to put them off.

                     GIT
         But I don't wanna, what if I hit
         something?

                    BUNNY
         It's just a warning, Git . . . It's nothing.

                   GIT (forlorn)
         Ah Jesus, Bunny, Jesus . . .

BUNNY sees the Cork van coming in the rear-view mirror.

> BUNNY
> They're coming, Git. (Short pause.) Just
> do what you did in the carpark. (Short
> pause.) Just do what you did. (Short
> pause.) Are you gonna do it?

Their rear windscreen shatters. They swerve.

> BUNNY
> Jesus Christ! Git! Come on! They're
> gonna kill all of us. You don't have to
> kill them for fuck's sake! Just shoot at
> them!

Pause. There are shots behind them.

> BUNNY
> Please! (Shakes his head.)

Pause. GIT lowers his window and stands up, out of it.

> BUNNY
> What are you doing?

150   EXT. SPEEDING CAR C EARLY MORNING

GIT sits out on the door.

151   EXT. CORK VAN EARLY MORNING

One of the CORK MEN is leaning out the window, firing at the car.

152   EXT. SPEEDING CAR C EARLY MORNING

GIT slowly takes aim.

153   INT. CAR C EARLY MORNING

BUNNY is trying to keep an eye on the road while appealing to GIT.

> BUNNY
> What are you doing? Come on!

154   EXT. SPEEDING CAR C EARLY MORNING

GIT aims carefully while the car bumps and jostles him.

The CORK MAN fires from the van. There is a sense of purpose about GIT.

155   INT. CORK VAN EARLY MORNING

As one CORK MAN fires, the DRIVER looks at GIT.

156   EXT. SPEEDING CAR EARLY MORNING

GIT fires once.

157   INT. CORK VAN EARLY MORNING

The windscreen shatters in on top of the two men. They are covered in glass. The driver can't see.

158   EXT. ROAD EARLY MORNING

The van slows down and drives into a ditch.

159   EXT. SPEEDING CAR C EARLY MORNING

GIT lowers the pistol. He keeps looking back. And finally climbs back into the car.

160   INT. CAR C EARLY MORNING.

GIT sits subdued, holding the pistol.

                        BUNNY
          That was good shooting.

GIT just looks out the window. Pause. .

                        BUNNY
          And don't worry about settling up. We
          can sort it out when this is all over.

                        GIT
          . . . What?

                        BUNNY
          What we agreed . . .

                        GIT
          About what?

                        BUNNY
          Don't make me do this, come on, you
          pay what you shoot. Six hundred.

                     GIT (pause)
          Are you joking?

                        BUNNY
          Why would I joke about something like
          that? I only make a joke when it's
          really funny. You should know that
          about me.

                        GIT
          But you were telling me to shoot.

                              BUNNY
                No. I was telling you to do what was
                right in that situation. What the right
                thing to do was.

                              GIT
                To shoot the gun.

                              BUNNY
                That's what the right thing happened
                to be. But it doesn't affect our
                agreement. Which you freely entered
                into. I don't want to have to be
                teaching you about ethics on top of
                everything else. Don't make me do
                that. (Pause.) Okay?

Pause. GIT is ignoring him.

                              BUNNY
                Okay? (Pause.) Another thing you can
                do, is buy it off me. We say . . . seven
                hundred, and I don't charge you for
                firing mine.

161   EXT. SECLUDED AREA DAY.

GIT opens the boot. FRANK blinks up at him.

                              GIT
                Where are we going?

162   EXT. WOODLAND DAY

The car drives on an overgrown trail.

163   INT. CAR C DAY

GIT, BUNNY and FRANK. FRANK is bound in the back.

                              FRANK
                Lads. I'm sitting on glass.

Pause.

                Sounded a bit hairy back there.

Pause.

                You not talking to me?

Pause.

                I can understand that. I didn't want to
                let yous down. It's just. The man was
                trying to kill me. Anybody can panic.

86

Turn left here. Yous have been very
good to me. I never wanted to be any
trouble. But life goes that way, you
know? There's all sorts of things.

164   EXT. WOODLAND TRAIL DAY

GIT holds FRANK by the arm. FRANK is still bound. BUNNY walks on in
front of them.

                          GIT
          What is this?

                          FRANK
          Me and French have things hidden in
          these woods. And that's what we're
          here to do. (Short pause.) And that's
          the simple beauty of it.

165   EXT. WOODS MORNING

It is misty. Up ahead, they see a footbridge over a small stream.

                          FRANK
          This is it.

They stop on the bridge. GIT and BUNNY look around, lighting cigarettes.

                          BUNNY
          Where is he?

                          FRANK
          He'll be here. (Short pause.) You
          getting nervous?

                          BUNNY
          No I'm not fucking . . . getting . . .
          nervous.

BUNNY glares at FRANK and then winks at GIT.

                          BUNNY
          Here this'll kill the time.

BUNNY offers FRANK his upraised thumb.

                          BUNNY
          Squeeze that as hard as you can.

                          FRANK
          I beg your pardon?

                          BUNNY
          Squeeze that as hard as you can. Come
          on, I'm not gonna hurt you.

Pause. FRANK grabs BUNNY'S thumb.

> BUNNY
> Ah Jaysus . . . hard as you can. Come
> on. (Short pause.) Right. Now do it with
> the other one.

> FRANK
> The other thumb?

> BUNNY
> No not the other thumb, you fucking . . .
> My . . . you squeeze it with the other
> hand now.

> FRANK
> Oh, the . . .

FRANK grabs BUNNY'S thumb with his other hand. BUNNY looks at GIT
with an expression that is verging on gleeful triumph.

> BUNNY
> Now I know something about you.

> FRANK
> Yeah?

> BUNNY
> Oh yeah.

FRANK makes a wanking motion on BUNNY'S thumb.

> FRANK
> And what do you know? What would
> that be?

> BUNNY (disgusted, deflated)
> Ah, you . . . bastard!

GIT laughs.

> FRANK
> You'd want to get up a bit earlier than
> that to catch me.

> BUNNY
> I'd never heard that before.

BUNNY'S expression changes when he sees TOM FRENCH standing in the
mist at one end of the bridge. Pause. FRENCH is very still for a moment
and then he comes towards them, his shoes clunking on the bridge. The
atmosphere is very different.

> TOM
> How are the men?

GIT and BUNNY nod, smoke their cigarettes. TOM and FRANK shake
hands.

                    TOM
You're some bollocks, do you know
that?

                   FRANK
I know everything.

                    TOM
You probably think you fucking do and
all. Bunny . . .

                   BUNNY
Tom.

                    TOM
How are you, Git? Nice few days?

                    GIT
When you . . . do . . . whatever this is.
(Short pause.) Are we quits?

                    TOM
Anto's already gone home. (Short
pause.) Okay?

                    GIT
But with me and you.

                    TOM
We'll see how things go. (Short pause.)
That's as good as my promises get.
That right, Frank?

              FRANK (derision)
Promises . . . State a you . . .

                    TOM
But the thing is, lads, we're not here to
fucking . . . my moral fibre. What way
d'you wanna do this?

                   FRANK
Long as it's done I'm easy.

                   BUNNY
For once . . .

                    TOM
Okay, why doesn't Git come with me?
I'm not armed. (Short pause.) I'll even
let Bunny search me, if he promises
not to enjoy it too much. (Raises arms.)
Sorry you don't like that.

BUNNY steps forward and searches TOM. TOM regards the others
confidently.

                            TOM
          Okay?

BUNNY nods.

                            TOM
          Be five minutes.

TOM begins to walk into the woods. GIT looks at FRANK and BUNNY and
then follows TOM.

                            BUNNY
          Git . . .

GIT turns. BUNNY makes a gun shape with his hand. GIT opens his
jacket, he still has BUNNY's pistol. BUNNY nods.

166   EXT. WOODS DAY

        TOM and GIT walk through the woods.

                            TOM
          Yous fucked me up, d'you know that?

Pause.

                            GIT
          Good.

                            TOM (laughs)
          What's in this for you?

                            GIT
          What.

                            TOM
          What the fuck are you going around
          saving little weasels like Grogan for?

GIT shrugs.

                            TOM (laughs)
          You're a soft touch. I betcha he played
          yous like a fucking piano.

Pause.

                            GIT
          Like you did and all?

                            TOM
          Ah now here, I was saving yous the
          hass. You didn't need to know what
          was going on. What difference was it
          gonna make to you? Think about it.
          Cunt's a thief.

GIT

Is this about plates?

TOM

Aah. The famous plates. Frank's a nice
fella, but you can't believe a word he
says. So you learn to hate him. For your
own good.

GIT

He said something about your wife.

TOM

Well. I don't want to be rude. But that's
between me and her.

167   EXT. A SMALL CLEARING DAY

TOM goes to a tree, points to a little notch.

TOM

This is it. I'm fucked if I'm digging.
You're young. Give us a fag.

TOM sticks the spade in the ground. GIT gives TOM a cigarette.

GIT

What is it?

TOM

About two foot down there's a suitcase.

GIT begins to dig.

TOM

You used to be with Sabrina Bradley,
didn't you?

Pause.

TOM

I've known her all her life. D'you know
that? (Pause.) Mm. She used to come in
with her little shorts. Skinny little legs.
Child grows up. Enters the adult world.
Behaving like an adult. I'm very fond of
her. (Short pause.) She's always had a
sneaky regard for me.

GIT stops digging, looks at TOM.

GIT

I doubt it.

GIT continues digging. TOM laughs.

91

                         TOM
              Hit a nerve there. You're a bit of an
              oddball, aren't you? You just, you don't
              talk to anybody. What do you do?
              What's in your life? Things like this?

                         GIT
              Just tryna stay outta the way.

                         TOM
              But that's where you're wrong. You
              need people doing you favours and
              shit. You shoulda been working for me
              a long time ago. Fucking bunch a
              morons I have.

                         GIT
              I don't work for you.

                         TOM
              Free country.

GIT hits the case.

                         TOM
              Da dah . . . Remember this. You're
              about as close as losers ever get to that
              kind of money.

GIT pulls the case out. TOM takes the case.

168   EXT. THE FOOTBRIDGE DAY

As GIT and TOM approach the bridge they can just hear the end of a
'conversation' between BUNNY and FRANK.

                         BUNNY
              Just shut the fuck up. You're like a
              fucking . . . Jesus, fucking . . .

                         TOM
              Flying form, Frank, yeah?

                         FRANK
              Nobody talks anymore.

169   EXT. WOODS DAY

FRANK leads GIT, BUNNY and TOM down by a stream.

                         TOM
              They were gonna build all around here
              a few years ago, Frank. That woulda
              shook you.

> FRANK (feigning huge interest)
> Well that's the luck a the draw, and
> it's just gas, isn't it? It really is. (Short
> pause.) I hope you boys are paying
> attention to this. See what money does
> to people? Forces them apart. I've
> never seen money bring anyone
> together and that's the truth.

> TOM
> That's an odd combination, Frank. You
> and the truth.

They reach a clearing.

> FRANK
> It's here.

> TOM
> I don't dig.

Pause.

> BUNNY
> Git's got the spade.

> GIT
> Is it far down?

> FRANK
> Not far.

170   EXT. THE CLEARING DAY

GIT is digging. He is up to his waist.

> FRANK
> Soil settles. Mmm.

> GIT
> There's something here.

> FRANK
> That's right.

GIT hands a box up to FRANK. FRANK takes a bundle from it and unwraps
it. It is a counterfeit plate. GIT notices he is standing on something.
Canvas. He pulls at it. It is big. BUNNY helps him. It is a bag with human
remains. They lay it on the ground.

> FRANK
> That's that then.

> TOM
> Sonny Mulligan.

Pause.

                            GIT
                    Did yous kill him?

                            TOM
                    Stupid thick tried to rob us.

                            FRANK (derision)
                    Money . . .

                            BUNNY
                    What happened?

                            TOM
                    Clash of personalities.

                            FRANK
                    Not with Sonny.

                            TOM
                    No. Sonny was a gent.

171   INT. SPEEDING CAR D DAY

YOUNG TOM, YOUNG FRANK and SONNY are speeding down a street,
pulling off balaclavas. They are in high spirits. They open cans of Double
Diamond beer.

                            TOM (V/O)
                    The counterfeit plates for Sonny's
                    retirement plan. Finest plates ever
                    made. Never seen craftsmanship like
                    it. He'd hired them from the big boys
                    across the water on condition that he
                    wouldn't print more than fifty grand.

171A   INT. WAREHOUSE NIGHT

A close shot of a pair of counterfeit plates being carefully cleaned after
use. Ink on a soft cloth. Slow tracking shot across stacks of twenty-dollar
bills in a suitcase. A hand places a final bundle in.

172   INT. WEDDING RECEPTION NIGHT

This is a flashback. YOUNG TOM, YOUNG FRANK and SONNY MULLIGAN
are at a wedding reception. YOUNG TOM has just got married. There is a
huge sense of celebration. Money has been spent. Champagne flows. The
photo is taken of FRANK, TOM and SONNY, that GIT has. A slow powdery
flash which dissolves into the next flashback.

                            FRANK (V/O)
                    Twenty-five years ago we were one of
                    the most successful gangs around.
                    We were very close. We had it all.
                    Tom even married Sonny's niece, and
                    I let him.

173   INT. WEDDING RECEPTION NIGHT

YOUNG TOM is having a row with SONNY. SONNY is trying to get him to sit down. YOUNG TOM pushes SONNY'S hands away.

> TOM (V/O)
> But we blew it. We wanted him to print
> a lot more than fifty grand. I'd a
> blazing row about it the week before
> he died, right in the middle of me own
> fucking wedding. All Sonny's pals
> there and all.

174   INT. CAR D NIGHT

YOUNG FRANK and YOUNG TOM driving. Following a car.

> FRANK (V/O)
> So we had the fantastic brainwave of
> borrowing the plates behind Sonny's
> back and printing our own sneaky
> batch.

175   EXT. WOODS NIGHT

We see YOUNG TOM watching SONNY. SONNY puts a plate in a case. Then he puts a pistol in, and buries the case.

> TOM (V/O)
> He always kept one on him. I saw
> where he buried the other one. The
> plan was, we'd print one side and do
> the other later.

176   EXT. WOODS NIGHT

SONNY is walking down a trail to his car. He approaches YOUNG FRANK from behind. YOUNG FRANK is hiding behind a tree.

> FRANK (V/O)
> If he knew what we were doing. Well,
> you could forget about it.

YOUNG FRANK is startled. SONNY begins to smile with recognition, puzzled.

YOUNG FRANK draws his pistol. SONNY is startled. FRANK shoots SONNY. SONNY sits, unconscious, slumped forward a little. Pause. YOUNG FRANK is sorry. He goes and sees if he can help him. He feels something. Searches. The other plate.

177   EXT. WOODS NIGHT

YOUNG TOM hears shots. He looks around, remembering the spot and
then runs away through the woods.

178   EXT. WOODS NIGHT.

YOUNG FRANK buries SONNY's body.

179   INT. CAR D NIGHT

YOUNG TOM and YOUNG FRANK sit in a car outside a bar. They have a
talk which develops into a row.

                         TOM (V/O)
              The Mulligans wanted to know what'd
              happened to Sonny. The big boys
              wanted their plates back. So we said
              Sonny'd ripped us off and
              disappeared. There was a lot of heat.
              We were very lucky not to be killed
              ourselves.

                         FRANK (V/O)
              And then, to top it all, Tom caught me
              in bed with his wife. We couldn't even
              breathe the same air anymore, let
              alone do a deal. Right up to here we
              are, a quarter of a century later.

YOUNG FRANK gets out of the car and storms off. YOUNG TOM sits on
his own.

180   EXT. WOODS DAY

We are back in the present. TOM, FRANK, GIT and BUNNY are standing
around the grave.

                         BUNNY
              Poor cunt lying out here in the cold all
              these years.

                         FRANK
              Ah, he was a prick. Let's burn that and
              fuck off.

TOM opens the case and puts the two plates together, then he produces a
pistol from the case and points it at the others. They are startled.

                         FRANK
              What are you doing?

                         TOM
              Where is she?

FRANK

Who?

TOM

Don't . . . fuck me around. Where
is she?

FRANK

Where's my twenty-five grand?

TOM

Just stop the shit, Frank. Where is she?

FRANK

She never showed.

Pause. TOM and FRANK look at each other, realisation dawning.

FRANK

I swear to God, Tom. She never came.

BUNNY

I'm fucking delighted. She did yous
both.

TOM cocks the pistol.

FRANK

There's no way that gun's gonna work
after twenty-three years.

BUNNY looks at GIT. GIT has BUNNY's pistol.

TOM

I like a gamble.

FRANK

Tom . . .

TOM shoots FRANK. FRANK falls into Sonny's grave. GIT and BUNNY step
back in shock.

TOM

And this is for fucking my wife.

TOM shoots FRANK again.

TOM (to BUNNY and GIT)
Where are yous going?

BUNNY

Just do it if you're gonna do it.

TOM

Is the faggot getting all catty?

BUNNY

I'm not that.

                                    TOM
                        You're not anything.

TOM points the gun at BUNNY. GIT takes his pistol and points it at TOM.
GIT pulls the trigger, the hammer hits an empty chamber. TOM shoots
BUNNY, wounding him in the shoulder, and turns on GIT. TOM'S gun does
not fire. GIT 'fans' the hammer and fires twice. TOM goes down.

Long pause. GIT, BUNNY, the bodies and smoke.

                                   BUNNY
                        I never thought I was the type.

Pause.

                                    GIT
                        What?

                                   BUNNY
                        I'm after shitting in my pants. (Pause.)
                        Why didn't you hit him the first time?

                                    GIT
                        Empty chamber.

                                   BUNNY
                        What were you doing with an empty
                        chamber?

                                    GIT
                        You told me always to leave one.

                                   BUNNY
                        No I didn't.

                                    GIT
                        I'm not arguing with you. You're a cunt.

+---+
| 'Sometimes the benefit of the doubt |
| can even save your life.' |
+---+

185   EXT. CLEARING DAY

GIT buries the bodies in Sonny Mulligan's grave. BUNNY sits against a
tree having a cigarette. He wears a makeshift sling. Blood spreads over it.
BUNNY is becoming weak, he opens the case.

                                   BUNNY
                        How much did French say we'd get for
                        these?

GIT looks quizzically at BUNNY's 'expertise.'

                                      98

                    GIT

I'd say you can get yourself another
pair of those white shoes.

                  BUNNY

You don't think a man would only have
one pair of shoes like them, do you?

                    GIT

Are you joking?

                  BUNNY

No. You'll know when I'm joking
because it's really funny.

GIT flattens the earth. BUNNY is getting weak. GIT goes to him. Picking
him up. Walking with BUNNY draped around him.

                    GIT

Come on Bun, you gotta stay awake for
me now. We get you sorted out. Keep it
together. Where are you going to go
after this. Come on tell me, what's the
plan, ha?

Pause.

                  BUNNY

Where are you going?

                    GIT

You're not coming with me.

                  BUNNY

Did I say I was? (Short pause.) I got
things to do.

                    GIT

Like I haven't?

                  BUNNY

I don't care what you fucking do. (Short
pause.) Long as you pay me for what
you fired.

                    GIT

I saved your life!

                  BUNNY

Fair enough. (Short pause.) I'll knock a
hundred off.

                    GIT

You want to sort out going to the
hospital before you do anything.

> BUNNY

Suppose . . . What am I gonna tell them?

> GIT

I'll say I did it.

> BUNNY

Will you?

> GIT

Would you fuck off?

Pause.

> BUNNY

Ah I'll pay some backstreet cunt.
(Pause.) It doesn't feel too bad anyway.
Like, I could drink a pint. You know
that way?

> GIT

Could you?

> BUNNY

Do you fancy that?

> GIT

Don't mind.

> BUNNY

Where d'you live?

> GIT

B&B.

> BUNNY

There's room in my house if you want,
till you get sorted out.

> GIT

Jaysus . . .

> BUNNY

You could have your own room. Thirty
pound a week, not too shabby.

> GIT

All this money in the bag, and you're
tryna get thirty quid off me.

> BUNNY

I always said it. If I ever got rich.
Wouldn't change me. And I'm gonna
stick to that.

> GIT

You're brilliant . . .

187   INT. SNOOKER HALL DAY

This is a dark place. SABRINA sits drinking a cup of coffee, smoking. She is lovely. BUNNY comes in, but this time he is barely recognisable. His wound has healed. He is well-dressed and groomed. He wears sunglasses. He comes and sits with SABRINA. They are in a secluded booth.

> BUNNY
> Thanks for coming.

> SABRINA
> That's alright. I haven't seen you
> around for a while.

> BUNNY
> I've been very busy. Going to go away
> I think.

> SABRINA
> Where are you going?

> BUNNY
> States.

Pause.

> SABRINA
> Do you know where Git went?

Pause. BUNNY takes an envelope and hands it to SABRINA.

> BUNNY
> Here.

> SABRINA
> What is it?

> BUNNY
> Put it away.

> SABRINA
> What is it?

> BUNNY
> Put it away.

> SABRINA
> What is it?

> BUNNY
> Would you put the fucking thing away
> when I tell you? Please . . .

SABRINA puts it away.

> SABRINA
>
> What is it?

> BUNNY (looks at her. Pause)
>
> It's a little few bob, for you and Head the Ball.

> SABRINA
>
> A few *bob*?

> BUNNY (derision about GIT)
>
> I know.

> SABRINA
>
> From who?

> BUNNY
>
> Ah, you know who. Don't make me say it.

Pause.

> SABRINA
>
> Git?

> BUNNY
>
> That may be who it is, yes.

> SABRINA
>
> Where is he?

> BUNNY
>
> He's gone away. To the States.

> SABRINA
>
> Do you think he knows anything about where Tom French is?

> BUNNY
>
> What would he know?

> SABRINA
>
> Anto told me Git was going to do something for him. To help Anto with a debt.

> BUNNY
>
> Yeah, well I think he mighta done that, alright. I heard that around. But I just bumped into him and he asked me to give you that.

SABRINA sees ANTO come in. He is hawking tickets.

                    SABRINA
You don't think he was involved
with . . . whatever happened to Tom
French, do you?

                    BUNNY
You must be joking love. Tom French is
after doing an insurance scam, and
fucked off. You mark my words. He's
done a Sonny Mulligan.

BUNNY goes to leave.

                    SABRINA
Bunny, wait!

BUNNY stops. SABRINA goes to him.

Pause.

                    SABRINA
If you . . . do . . . bump into him again.
Will you give him this for me?

She hands him the ring.

                    BUNNY (short pause)
I don't know, love. (Pause.) But I'll tell
you this. Whatever happens, in the
coming years. You be ready to forgive
your man. Because sometimes the
benefit of the doubt can even save your
life. I'm learning that. And so many
men (Short pause.) think so highly of
you, it might be hard for you to see
which one is the one that's going to
light up just from hearing your name.
(Pause.) But I've met him. And you
have too.

He kisses her cheek and leaves.

SABRINA looks around. ANTO is in an argument. He gets pushed.

188   EXT. STREET DAY

BUNNY comes out and crosses the road to a brand new BMW. He gets in.

188A   INT. CAR E DAY

GIT is in the driver's seat.

                    GIT
How'd it go?

103

                    BUNNY
          Jaysus, Git, not too good. But I
          managed to get this back off her.

He gives GIT the ring.

                    GIT
          What? I didn't want it! I wanted her to
          have it. . . . You fucking moron.

BUNNY is embarrassed. He is not sure what to say.

                    BUNNY
          We're gonna miss the plane.

GIT shakes his head and starts the car. He begins to laugh.

                    GIT
          What the *fuck* am I doing?

CREDITS.

After a minute we hear airport sounds and GIT and BUNNY's voices.

                    BUNNY
          What's the story?

                    GIT
          It's delayed. Another hour.

                    BUNNY
          Fucking typical. Get me another pint.

                    GIT
          I don't have any more Irish money.

                    BUNNY
          What? Ah for fuck's sake. (Pause.) Can
          I ask you something?

                    GIT
          Depends what it is.

                    BUNNY
          Just, it's been bothering me for a while.
          On my mind . . .

                    GIT
          What is it?

                    BUNNY
          Just. D'you remember that bird you
          were with that night in the hotel?

                    GIT
          Yeah . . .

BUNNY
Did she suck your cock?

GIT
That's what's been on your mind?

BUNNY
You know . . . I reflect . . . about things.
Did she?

GIT
Mmhm.

BUNNY
Yeah?

GIT
But I went down, as well. (Short pause.)
I always do.

Peter McDonald as Git Hynes

APPENDICES

Director Paddy Breathnach, Executive Producer Mark Shivas
and Producer Robert Walpole during filming

APPENDIX 1
Synopses of Drafts One and Two

As the script for *I Went Down* was developed each draft tended to be radically different. In fact the story is different in each draft. This is an outline of previous stories. What then follows in Appendix II is a discussion between the writer, producer and director concerning how it developed and why. Appendix III contains examples of scenes from these previous discarded drafts.

Draft One

The screenplay begins with a discussion in Tom French's bar the morning after a fight between a local young man Christopher 'Git' Hynes and Tom French's nephew, Johnner Doyle. Johnner has been badly hurt and Tom French demands compensation or swift revenge. At the meeting with Git is his mother's lover, Darren. Darren appeals to French, asking for clemency. French gives Git one week to come up with ten thousand pounds. Git, a petty thief, has no money and has to consider stealing it somewhere, something which Darren strongly advises him against. But Git is very proud, to the point of recklessness.

In this draft he is quite a belligerent, pushy character who is still sniffing around his ex-girlfriend, Sabrina. She is heavily pregnant, but her present partner is serving a prison sentence. Git is trying to woo her again.

Git solicits the help of his boyhood friend, Anto McQuigly. Anto is an expert car thief. He agrees to drive a getaway for one job, a robbery on a post office.

Git hires a gun from a man who remains nameless. This scene has its similar version in the final draft where Bunny teaches Git about his revolver.

The early Bunny character is called Jimmy Kelly. He is a local hard man and seasoned armed robber who is now very down on his luck. Git goes to him for advice but ends up with Jimmy inveigling himself into the job. Anto is very apprehensive about Jimmy.

109

His instincts are right. The job is a disaster. Customers in the post office are terrorised and beaten by Jimmy. The trio escape with a bag of two pence coins. Jimmy tells Git not to be disheartened. He has another plan, which is to hold a wealthy family hostage while using a family member to withdraw cash from their bank. Git agrees as long as no one gets hurt. Anto agrees to help Git one more time.

Jimmy does some reconnaissance. Git is abducted by vigilantes, beaten and warned to cease his petty thievery. These vigilantes are acquaintances of Darren and have terrorist connections. Git berates Darren for interfering. Darren protests that he is trying to do what's best for Git.

Git continues to sniff around Sabrina. They make love.

Jimmy has spotted his target family on the Southside of Dublin, a family called Reynolds. The gang gain entry in the evening and hold the family hostage with a view to stealing their money in the morning. Needless to say, things go awry and Jimmy runs amok. Anto gets into a fight with him and Git has to calm the situation.

The following morning they manage to extort some money from the Reynolds, but draw attention to themselves and are pursued by the guards. Jimmy fires at the guards and is shot in the head, but remarkably survives. The gang escape thanks to Anto's driving.

Git attempts to give Tom French his money, but Tom French has in turn been terrorised by Darren's vigilante/terrorist friends. Git is then assaulted by French but told to keep the money. Git makes a sort of peace with Sabrina and goes out drinking cans of lager in the street.

Draft Two

Tom French is losing his grip on his little neighbourhood empire. He's afforded protection to businesses in the area for years, but as he and his cohorts have grown older they've let their authority slide. One of the prime nuisances is a petty criminal, Git Hynes.

French threatens Hynes and orders him to pay ten thousand pounds worth of damages so he can reimburse local business for damage to their property and theft after a recent wave of burglary.

In this draft Git is actually living with Sabrina and they have a child. Again Git gets help from Anto and Jimmy, and although their initial crime spree is equally disastrous the situations are more comic. As in the final draft their problems arise from their technical inabilities. But they stay in Dublin, and the Anto character features throughout. There is a constant tension between Jimmy and Anto, which Git keeps having to defuse.

Their problems come to a head when, in an attempt to rob a betting shop, they interrupt a poker game between several hard criminal bosses, including Tom French. They steal the money from the poker game, but panic that they have been recognised.

Git tries to return the money, but in the end manages successfully to blackmail Tom French into leaving him in peace by using information his father furnishes him with from prison, where he is serving a life sentence.

APPENDIX 2
Genre, Pace and Landscape

*A conversation between Conor McPherson, Paddy Breathnach
and Robert Walpole, 6 August 1997*

Conor   I met you when you came back from Cannes in May 1995. Had you made a decision about the type of film you wanted to do next?

Paddy   We had probably made a decision a good while before that, but because we were involved in producing a documentary series which was paying for the company and which was outside Dublin, we weren't really around from January until Cannes. But we had seen your play [*The Good Thief*] in October and we were both really impressed. At that stage we were trying to formalise the company and I remember at one point we were saying to ourselves, 'What the fuck are we doing here? We've seen this play. We know this is a really good writer. We're really interested in him and it's two or three months later and we haven't done anything about it!' But we were caught up with the *WRH*[1] thing.

So when we came back from Cannes we said, 'OK, we've done our stuff paying the overhead for the year. We're in a good position. We really have to push ahead and get this film going.'

Conor   So you had a pretty definite idea about the type of film you wanted to make? Or was it more like a vague direction?

Paddy   I certainly think I wanted to go into the realm of genre. As things developed and we started talking a lot more I think that began to refine itself and also we reacted against things that were happening in the film world at the time.

112

There were an awful lot of 'Hood' movies coming out, tough-guy neighbour-hood-type films. We may have considered starting out in that direction but there were so many of them we felt we had probably missed that boat. So I think we all became involved in a reactive process of finding our territory.

I think a point came where we knew we wanted to do a film that was crime-based and possibly revenge-based. And I remember we began to talk about making it expansive, to get it out of one locale, to spread it across a journey. So there was an element of quest about the film.

Conor   I think that's how the story developed. You were concerned we didn't keep the events limited to one particular world. It starts in one place and ends in another.

Paddy   I think that's right. Once we weren't concerned with creating one particular kind of world, the film became more character-led. For instance we seized upon the explosiveness of the Jimmy character, who later became Bunny, a quality that Git had quite early on too. As their relationship grew through the development process they naturally became more polarised in what they represented. But it was their personalities which were beginning to primarily interest us.

Rob   I think Bunny's development through the writing process is a good way of tracking how the whole thing developed. At the very beginning Jimmy, as he was called then, was a real headbanger. He was a hard, gross kind of unattractive character who wandered around the house in stained tracksuits, hitting his kids. Generally he was a bit scummy.

There was a scene in the first draft where Git and Anto come to him precisely because he is a psycho, a one-dimensional hard man. When they call he's on the toilet. As he comes down to Git and Anto he slaps one of his kids and says, 'Go up and flush that.' Now to see the development of that character in the first draft to the more fumbling, big-hearted but no less explosive or aggressive Bunny Kelly in the final film, for me represents the movement of the whole process.

Conor   So was there a feeling it was the kind of film which appeals to a wide audience, or were you trying to capture something purely about the Republic of Ireland?

Paddy   I think we all shared a gut instinct to move away from a lot of the clichés, the things that were reappearing in all Irish films. You know, the guilt-ridden nation, the IRA storylines, people who are always pissed out of their heads, horses, all those things . . . And that you definitely couldn't have sex with someone from your own country and enjoy it!

We were aware of all those clichés, and we wanted to just get rid of them, because they were boring. I remember sometimes bits of those things began to creep in and we'd try to take them out again. But the interesting thing is that it's hard to escape out of all that. But I do feel in a funny way that we've taken all the clichés away, but it still feels like an Irish film in many respects.

Conor Something that strikes me when I look at the early drafts is that it's centrally about one character. I found in the beginning that it was easier, lazier, I suppose, to have a hero with an eventful life who we follow everywhere. But as we progressed it became a story about relationships between characters who are given equal weight. Were you concerned with the singular nature of the first things I wrote for you?

Paddy I think so. We had some experience of the film world but I'm not sure we were massively ahead of you. You were coming in. You had decided to be a full-time writer. And maybe you weren't even sure just what that meant. And we were earning our living in the film business but had limited experience of developing scripts. You were giving us stuff which we felt was fantastic and had huge potential, but you come to a point where you have to make a decision. How long do you let something grow, building ideas with the freshness, rawness and naturalness of somebody's talent before you say, 'Okay, let's shape it. Let's come in and influence it.' And it's a very thin line.

And I know that from your point of view there was once or twice where it was very frustrating for you. Sometimes we'd bat things down after you'd worked very hard on a draft. We'd come in sometimes with the jackboots on. Not necessarily aggressively but perhaps a bit belligerently. But it's a problem you have to recognise, at what point do you decide to shape something? How long do you let it breathe and live?

Conor So at what point did you decide you were getting what you wanted?

Paddy We were at a point for a long time where the set-up was really strong. But the world of the film and the rest of the plot we weren't quite getting. The set-up was so strong it offered us the choice of any number of genres we could have progressed into. But there is a point of discovery where you decide exactly what you're interested in. It was November or December 1995 when I knew we had to get it out of a 'neighbourhood' and away from a familiar set of 'characters'. I wanted to get it out from that world. At that stage three of them went on a journey, Git, Anto and Bunny. But the journey you put them on was from the Northside of Dublin to the Southside! I think I had something more expansive in mind!

114

Laughter

Conor   So there was a slight misunderstanding . . .

Laughter

Paddy   Maybe, yeah . . .

Rob   I think all the time it was getting bigger. My memories of the early drafts are that they're very hard, very much like a TV movie set in North Dublin. There's some great writing there and some stuff that came through to the final draft. But it was never going to create a world that was interesting to people outside Ireland. As the story moved away from Dublin to different places it developed . . . it took on a lot more heart. It wasn't just a geographical journey. Whereas in the first draft these Northsiders are uncomfortable on the Southside – there's a marvellous scene where they're in a supermarket full of products they don't recognise – the final draft creates a wider journey where Git and Bunny just aren't comfortable anywhere. And especially not in the criminal underworld. But the first draft stopped any possibility of further journeying. Once they got into the hostage situation it became very hard. There was some really funny writing. But it didn't have much heart.

Paddy   The humour you can have in the theatre can sometimes be created out of tension. A live audience sharing an experience can be prompted to laugh at things they mightn't normally think of as funny. But in the cinema if you go down a dark road – you go down a dark road. Maybe in an American landscape – Tarantino can sometimes do it – something cruel can be funny. But I feel in this landscape I just wouldn't have been able to do that.
   Now maybe I'm wrong. Maybe it's about expanding your horizons.

Conor   I think a time came where a conscious decision was made – or maybe I just finally accepted – to push for the comedy, which resulted in characters who were a lot more heartfelt. By the time I was writing the third draft, we were ostensibly looking for good jokes, good comic situations and good visual slapstick. When I was working in the office we were chucking ideas around, things people had thought of on the way to work. Things which would, we hoped, definitely entertain people. And so even though, for example, we have ended up with a form of hostage situation, it's now full of irony in that the hostage is almost keeping his captors prisoner because he's canny enough to hold onto his information and sort of drip-feed them lies.

Paddy   He's inflicting pain on them.

Conor   And it's interesting, when you push for something humorous, you often end up with something which is somehow more intriguing. Things sort of take on more meaning.

Paddy   Yeah. Something which became very central to the story later on was this idea of the characters being inarticulate. And I know that this element was something very close to your heart. I think we seized on it and exploded it out a lot more. Where did that come from for you?

Conor   I think it comes from striving for something that's truthful. If Bunny suddenly made a big eloquent speech in the film, what we might call an actor's 'Oscar Chance,' it'd distract the audience. Simply because we can't accept that a man of such intelligence could possibly have ended up in such a stupid situation. What interests me is that we have a man who *thinks* he's intelligent and he needs to learn that he's not as clever as he thinks he is. In other words, he has a lack of humility.

And this gives us a lot of comedy. For instance, whenever Bunny tries to justify his actions or list reasons for doing something. He'll say the same thing three times in a row without realising it. He pushes forward to the end of a hopelessly repetitive argument.

Paddy   And his energy is so sincere.

Conor   His journey becomes one of accepting his limitations. By the end of the film he accepts that he can learn things from Git. But Git has also learned to trust Bunny. We have a man of action, Bunny, and a man of reasonableness, Git. Bunny has unpremeditated knee-jerk responses. Git's responses are more considered. But neither of them solely working upon their own instincts separately can ever achieve anything. Bunny nearly lands them both in prison in the first few minutes of their journey because of his impulse to steal. But Git almost gets himself killed trying to save Grogan. It's only Bunny's protection that saves him.

So their journey is one of learning to trust each other's natural skills. And this is done I think through humorous episodes where we see their gifts and their shortcomings displayed for us rather than through articulate self-awareness on their part. But I don't think I was entirely conscious of that when I was writing it. I really only kind of see it in retrospect.

Paddy I think something which also influenced the story was a concern to give all the right genre signals with the landscape we had available to us. I know that during the time you worked here in the office we began to speak a lot in terms of plant and payoff. I mean we began to talk in that language all the time. And if an idea came up, we were immediately reacting to it like, 'Oh there's a payoff later on that we can get if we want to.' And there were so many gags actually that we were dropping things out. There was so much stuff we were filling it up. There was too much.

Conor We were slowing it down.

Paddy Yeah.

Conor In fact the question of sustaining pace became very important. We've published the entire screenplay here but there are scenes missing from the final cut, scenes which were actually shot. Was it necessary to cut them because the film might lose momentum?

Paddy There were two conversations between Sabrina and Git on the phone. One was at the petrol station and one was at the hotel. The first one was cut because so much stuff had been set up at the beginning of the film, fantastic stuff, that when Git and Bunny get on the road we need to keep them moving. We need to spend time with them as quickly as possible. Git ringing Sabrina just seemed to slow the film down there. Now, that might be to do with the way I shot it on the day. We did an awful lot of set-ups that day at the petrol station. I can remember the bond company looking at my schedule in preproduction. And they said, 'Well, you know, twenty-four set-ups in a day, you know, it's an awful lot to do.' But I said, 'Well, I *can* do it!'

Laughter

Paddy And it's not about whether you *can* do it. It's really about whether you *should*. And I might have been able to play with the scene and get more tension out of it if I had listened at that time.

The second phone call at the hotel came after quite a few dialogue scenes where the characters had been quite revealing. At this point the characters are going to relax for a while. It felt too much like we were changing down a gear and then reverting back too quickly. Again it felt more important for Git and Bunny to be together. And somehow the phone call stopped that happening as easily. Not in

117

terms of meaning or themes, but purely in terms of momentum. For me it was a pity because I felt that particular scene had some of the best direction, some of the best cinematography in the film. Antoine Byrne who plays Sabrina, and indeed Pete, they were fantastic. There was a lovely tension in the frame and also there was fantastic lighting on Antoine at the end of the shot. But I had to lose it because the overall momentum needs to win out at that stage and you have to let it.

Rob What I find really interesting about this is that even in one scene, the scene between Git and Bunny in the bar for instance, cuts are made which move it on. In the film it ends up inverted and much shorter.

Paddy Well something that struck me and Emer[2] was that the better the writing is, the easier it is to cut because the ideas are clear and the emotions are clear, so we can say 'Okay, we're just taking this part and dealing with that.' You find that the level of emotional narrative clarity is so strong that you can actually take things away from it. The reason we cut was because, and these scenes are printed in full in the screenplay, the scene with Git and Bunny in the bar and the scene where Git tells the girl about his father, back to back in the cut they were probably like eleven or twelve minutes long. But now they're about four minutes. And I'd say, if you look at the rushes you'd be completely enthralled with the dialogue and the performances, but when you see them in the overall thing you'd say well we've given them what we need to know and now it's time to move on. The hunger is for the payoffs from the stuff we've established. We have to push on and let people know what's going to happen with these things.

Rob Another place where a cut was made like that was where Git and Bunny are chasing after Frank to the other hotel. There's a very funny moment where the characters reflect about the previous night. It's nothing to do with the chase. It's nothing to do with the drama, but Bunny is saying, 'This is what I'd rather reflect on . . . ' It worked really well, the performances are really good, it was shot really nicely, but it's a detour and it slowed it down.

Conor And that's a rhythm you find when you're editing . . .

Paddy I think that's probably true. But it's still got something to do with the relationship between genre and landscape. Say if the chase was happening in the desert in Arizona – and they stop to make a phone call – the sense of greater distance is going to have an impact. You can use that feeling of space, the opportunities to pause are better. But when you're on those roads in rural Ireland, you don't have that sense of isolation to the same extent. Now maybe you can create that. Maybe I could have done more to create that. But the fact is that the film is very full anyway. There's so much that we threw in there, it's very big and explosive, some things just had to go out of that. I wonder if we were to go back and say, 'Let's muster up the energy to rewrite it- do another draft,' maybe we'd know this time to leave things out at the writing stage.

Conor   I think I learned that you come to a stage where you have to stop. You have to accept that this is what the film is about. If you're not happy, start again somewhere else. You decide at a certain stage that this draft, even though it may be too long, too short, whatever, 'This draft represents the film that I want to make.' And you continue writing it in terms of the genre you think it fits. If it's a thriller, you'll know pretty quickly whether the pace is right or not. If it's a comedy, it better be funny. Or if it's simply a story about some characters, are they interesting, do we like them and so on. Those are important decisions. Because they help you to cut what you don't need.

Paddy; This film was developed through a reactive process. We were reacting to what you were writing and trying to hone and define with you. I think in the future I would try to reach a sort of meta-position much earlier. Like what you're saying about the big decisions. To reach an objective position where you're focused on the core issues you really want to develop.
    You see it can be a problem when the writing is very good. You can be bamboozled by good writing. You can go with something a lot longer than you should.

Conor   Because you've lost sight . . .

Paddy   You've lost sight of something that's central. But I have to say that the aspect of writing that last draft where it was quite public, I think was an amazing thing and a remarkable thing. To have that line where the script transfers from writer to producer and director over a six week period where you're living with the script as it's coming out, the line of transfer from one to the other, those conversations allow you as a director to immerse yourself in the film at a much earlier stage. So that when you get into preproduction you've subsumed so much.

Rob   The notion of coming into an office and being very public about the process of writing and being open, as soon as you had four or five new pages, putting them on the table and saying, 'Are we going in the right direction with this?' That's what made this film happen in the space of time that it did. And it did happen very quickly. It's not like going off and writing in a vacuum, and you'd been through that, and it takes a while to react to a couple of months' work. It takes time to absorb it. And from a writer's point of view, you're waiting for a reaction.

Paddy   There's two levels. One is to read a whole script and react to it on a linear basis throughout. But the other level is meta thinking, blocking the whole plot out very coolly, deciding the core things we want *and what we like about the film* and how to bring those things out. So you end up with a rich bed of warm territory that you can then subsequently become analytical about, and apply structure to. It's certainly the approach I'll consider next time.

Conor   What next time?

---

[1]   *Waterford Regional Hospital*, a six part documentary series produced by Treasure Films. Broadcast by RTE 1995.

[2]   Emer Reynolds. Editor on *I Went Down*. Also cut Paddy's first feature, *Ailsa*.

APPENDIX 3
Scenes from Previous Drafts

1   Scenes 11 to 15 from First Draft
Git gets Anto to be his Driver

11   EXT. DAY. A STREET ON A CORPORATION ESTATE

A road runs along a green. There are groups of young people in knots on
the corner and outside gardens on the street. A stolen car is racing up and
down the street. The driver throws it into handbrake turns and
wheelspinning skids. The young people on the street cheer and egg him
on. Mothers pull their children in off the road. GIT sits on a wall with some
teenagers. He watches the car.

> GIT (to a TEENAGER)
> Is that Anto McQuigley?

> TEENAGER 1
> Yeah.

> TEENAGER 2
> He's a fuckin looper.

As the car skids around the corner of the green, a squad car pulls into the
estate with its lights flashing. People throw bricks and bottles at the squad
car. ANTO McQUIGLEY takes off. He bumps into the kerb and mounts the
green, heading for an exit in the estate but after mounting the green the
car stalls. The guards close in. ANTO puts the car into reverse and speeds
backwards around the green.

> TEENAGER
> What the fuck is he doing?

> GIT
> He can't get it into gear.

ANTO reverses furiously for a hundred yards with the engine racing. He crashes backwards into the pillar of a house and bolts from the car into the garden. He climbs over the garage roof.

> GIT (to TEENAGERS)
> See youse.

GIT runs down the road. The guards follow ANTO over the back roof.

12   EXT. GARDEN

GIT runs through a back garden into the back lane. ANTO sprints by him. GIT runs after him. The guards chase down the lane behind them.

> GIT
> Anto, stall.

> ANTO (panicking)
> Fuck off.

They run on.

> GIT
> I have to talk to you.

> ANTO
> This isn't a really good time, Git, you
> know what I mean?

They turn a corner.

> GIT
> I need a driver.

> ANTO
> Git, get lost or we're both dead.

> GIT
> Where are you going?

ANTO runs for another 50 metres panicking.

> ANTO
> I don't know.

GIT checks behind them and pulls ANTO through a back garden door which leads onto the lane.

13   EXT. GARDEN

In the garden is a long kennel with wire mesh. They tumble into the garden. GIT kicks the lane door closed.

14   EXT. GARDEN

They crawl into the kennel and crouch, trying to get their breath. The guards run by the garden. ANTO and GIT look at each other.

>   ANTO
>   Thanks.

GIT looks away.

>   ANTO
>   What do you need a driver for?

>   GIT
>   I need to get ten grand.

>   ANTO
>   What are you doing? A bank?

>   GIT
>   No. No banks.

>   ANTO
>   Git, I don't do that sort of stuff. I only
>   act the bollox. You know? For the doss.

>   GIT
>   Once I get the ten grand, everything
>   else is yours.

>   ANTO
>   It's not my bag Git.

>   GIT
>   I have to get it for Tom French.

>   ANTO
>   Aw for fucks sake Git. What are you
>   doing anything for that cunt for?

>   GIT
>   I don't have a choice.

>   ANTO
>   What are you going to do?

>   GIT
>   Anything. Petrol stations, post office,
>   no banks.

>   ANTO
>   We'd have to keep changing the
>   fucking car. I think you're out of your
>   fucking mind Git.

Pause.

>   GIT
>   Alright. I'll get someone else.

A squad car drives by the door to the lane. They both crouch down further.
Pause.

                        ANTO
            I'll do one or two. Just to get you
            started.

GIT looks at him.

                        GIT
            Thanks.

Pause.

                        ANTO
            It's alright. A fucking life of crime.

GIT smiles. In the darkness of the kennel they hear a low growl.

                        ANTO
            Jesus Christ!

A huge dog is baring its teeth and advancing slowly.

                        ANTO
            Git . . .

                        GIT
            Shh. . Come on doggy. Come on.

The dog is inches from them growling. Git suddenly strikes out and hits
the dog across the face with the revolver. The dog slumps to the ground
without a whimper.

                        ANTO
            Fucking hell . . . Did you kill it?

                        GIT
            I should fucking hope so.

He moves to get out of the kennel.

            (Continuing) Fucking dog . . .

15   INT. PUB. NIGHT

ANTO and GIT are drinking in a pub.

                        ANTO
            You ever done it before?

GIT shakes his head and looks away.

                        ANTO
            It's gonna be hard.

                        GIT
            I'm thinking about getting Jimmy Kelly.

                    ANTO (annoyed)
You're out of your fucking head. He'll
get us all killed.

                    GIT
I need someone who means business.

                    ANTO
You can't rely on him.

                    GIT
He's what we need. A total bollox.
That's what I'm relying on.

                    ANTO
Aw yeah, you can rely on him to be a
total bollox.

                    GIT
He's done it before.

                    ANTO
But you can't trust him.

                    GIT
I need a heavy.

                    ANTO
I don't, Git. We used to live across the
road from the Kelly's. Everyone'll tell
you he's mental. I saw him kick the
shit out of his own grandad one
Sunday morning. And then he put him
in a bin and left him there. People
were too scared to pull the poor aul
fucker out in case Jimmy came back.

                    GIT
Good. Look Anto, I'm not asking him to
be my best man. I just need a scary
bollox. I'm gonna be shitting it as it is.
I can't have anybody having a go.
Jimmy Kelly will save all that hassle.

ANTO shakes his head.

                    ANTO
I don't know why you're doing this.

GIT looks away.

          (Continuing) Git . . .

                    GIT
What.

                    125

ANTO

Go away for a year or two.

GIT shakes his head.

(Continuing) It'll all be forgotten about
when you get back.

GIT looks at ANTO.

GIT

I don't want it to be forgotten about.

Pause.

ANTO (drinks his pint)

I'll see you in the morning. We'll talk
to that mad Kelly bastard. But I don't
know who's worse; him or you.

He leaves. GIT looks round the bar and then drinks his pint.

2 Scenes 58 and 59 from First Draft

The Gang holds the Reynolds Family Hostage

58   INT. STUDY. NIGHT

MR REYNOLDS sits behind his desk. GIT sits in a chair to one side and JIMMY stands with his hands on his hips. It oddly resembles some form of interview or business meeting. MR REYNOLDS takes three bank books from a locked drawer and places them on the desktop.

> MR REYNOLDS
> There is one joint account.

> JIMMY
> You and your wife . . .

> MR REYNOLDS
> Yes.

JIMMY picks up the books.

> JIMMY
> These two are just you?

MR REYNOLDS nods. JIMMY leafs through the books. GIT watches him.

> JIMMY
> Can you take money out of the joint
> account on one signature?

> MR REYNOLDS
> Just my signature?

> JIMMY
> Yeah . . .

> MR REYNOLDS
> No, we need both signatures.

> JIMMY
> Do youse not trust each other?

MR REYNOLDS smiles.

> MR REYNOLDS
> I don't know. Just the way . . . it is.
> I don't know, we've had it for years.

> JIMMY
> Are you trying to be funny?

Pause.

MR REYNOLDS
No. it's just the way . . . My wife
opened the account.

JIMMY
Shut up!

Pause.

JIMMY
D'you like the ladies?

MR REYNOLDS
Sorry?

JIMMY
D'youse have office parties at
Christmas and all?

MR REYNOLDS
Christmas party, yes.

JIMMY
Is there nice birds in the office?

Pause.

Is there?

MR REYNOLDS looks at GIT and JIMMY.

MR REYNOLDS
What do you mean?

JIMMY
Do you ever bang your secretary on the
photocopier?

MR REYNOLDS smiles nervously.

MR REYNOLDS
No . . .

JIMMY
Then why are you going all red?

MR REYNOLDS shrugs.

JIMMY
Blokes like you make me want to puke.

Pause.

MR REYNOLDS
I'm sorry.

                    JIMMY
          Shut up!

JIMMY looks at GIT and motions with his head. They walk into the
hallway.

                    JIMMY (to MR REYNOLDS)
          I'm leaving this open. Don't fucking
          move. D'you hear me?

MR REYNOLDS nods.

59   INT. HALLWAY. NIGHT

JIMMY and GIT stand beside the study door.

                    JIMMY (indicating bankbooks)
          There's eight grand in this and eleven
          and a half in this. Okay. Big deal. But
          the joint account . . .

He hands the book to GIT.

          Sixty-seven *thousand* quid.

                    GIT
          Fuck . . .

                    JIMMY
          Let's think about this. We've got your
          ten grand covered. But Jesus, let's,
          let's, have a . . . fucking moment here.
          What about, now just for, for you know,
          because we're thinking about this.

                    GIT
          Okay.

                    JIMMY
          In the morning I take Fucko to these
          two banks, five grand here, five grand
          there. Ten grand. Okay. But, now, what
          if . . . we get him to ring *this* one and
          take Mr. *and* Mrs. down to this one. Ten
          grand for a *car* for one of the *kids* It's
          their *birthday* whatever. He rings the
          manager. Both of them go to the bank.
          In, out. You know Git. Sweeten it up . . .
          What do you think?

                    GIT
          I, you know . . . I want to . . . I want to
          sort you and Anto out. But it's a risk.
          You know?

                           129

> JIMMY
>
> Just get him to *ring*. See what they say.
> 'We've been with the bank for blah
> blah years . . . ' 'all our money . . . ' 'It's
> an emergency . . . we got to get this
> fucking *car* . . . ' Think about it.

Pause.

> This way me and Anto get paid. It's all
> out of your fuckin hair: we can *relax* a
> little bit.

Pause.

> Think about it.

GIT nods.

> JIMMY
>
> Alright?

> GIT
>
> We'll have to think about it, you know?

> JIMMY
>
> Good. This is just, you know?

> GIT
>
> Yeah. You're taking him to the bank.

> JIMMY
>
> I can do *his* two banks. Come back.
> Get her, we do the joint. Get back here.
> Split.

> GIT
>
> They're gonna see your face.

> JIMMY
>
> I can't wear this on the street. But!

He lifts his balaclava up and produces a false moustache and a pair of
sunglasses. He puts them on. GIT laughs.

> GIT
>
> You've got to be fucking joking.

> JIMMY
>
> I wish I was.

> GIT
>
> The fucking funny thing is – you *do*
> look completely different.

130

                    JIMMY
Well that's the idea.

                    GIT
You look stupid.

                    JIMMY
Wait til you see the wig.

                    GIT
The *wig?*

                    JIMMY
Don't laugh. Have to do it.

                    GIT
I know. Come on, we'll put him with
the rest

                    JIMMY
Okay. But Git. About the other.

He shakes a bank book and pulls his balaclava back down over his face.

                    JIMMY (continuing)
It's something to consider.

                    GIT
I know.

3   Scenes 19 to 22 from Second Draft

A Considerably Weaker Tom French Attempts to Intimidate Git.
Strangely Philosophical

9   EXT. DAY. BACK STREET.

There are one or two businesses in the area. Rag trade, wholesale
butcher's. JIM's car stops near a furniture dealer. A sign says 'Pat French.
Beds. Suites. Kitchenware. Trade only.'

20   INT.

JIM leads GIT into the main warehouse. It is wall-to-wall furniture, oddly
laid out with a certain coherence as though it were a huge open plan
studio flat. Bedrooms, living rooms, kitchens. They go up a staircase and
across a gantry overlooking the warehouse. They are high above it. Then
in a corridor with an office off it. The office is visible from the corridor,
partitioned with wood to waist height and glass to the ceiling. As they
walk to the door GIT can see TOM FRENCH on the phone. He sits on his
desk. Another man, TONY, sits in a chair near the desk. There is
surprisingly little in the office. Some chairs, tables, phones and a coffee
machine.

21   INT. OFFICE DAY.

GIT AND JIM ENTER.

> TOM (into phone)
> Yeah.

He motions GIT to sit down, and signals the coffee machine. JIMMY goes
to the coffee machine. TONY stares at GIT. GIT doesn't know where to
look.

> TOM (into phone)
> Yeah.

JIMMY hands GIT a mug of coffee.

> JIM
> There's no sugar.

> GIT
> Yeah. Great.

TONY stares at GIT. GIT concentrates on his coffee. JIM sits to one side.

> TOM (into phone)
> Both legs?

GIT listens.

                    TOM
          Mm. Well that's no use then. (Pause)
          Will you go back around? (Pause)
          Okay. Well you're only getting half
          your wages. (Pause) Yeah. Okay. Good
          man. See you on Friday.

TOM hangs up the phone.

                    TOM
          Now. (To JIM) Where's my coffee?

                JIM (getting up)
          Your coffee? I thought you meant him.

                    TOM
          What? Why am I giving him coffee and
          not having any myself?

                JIM (at machine)
          I dunno. I just, you know.

                TOM (to GIT)
          I'm not saying you can't have your
          coffee, son. Have it now.

                    GIT
          Thanks.

JIMMY hands TOM a mug of coffee.

                    TOM
          Now I have the stupid mug. Must've
          fucking come with a fucking Easter
          egg. Anyway.

          (To GIT) Ah. We got a new machine
          and eh. You know the . . . Ah we're
          playing with the fucking thing all the
          time. I must've had about nineteen
          cups of it today. I don't even want it.

He takes a drink.

          So what's the story? What are you
          doing with the car stereos. What is it?
          Chris or Git?

                    GIT.
          Whatever.

                    TOM
          What's the story?

                    133

                    GIT
What do you mean?

                    TOM
You gonna give it up?

Pause.

You gonna give it up?

                    GIT
I don't know what . . .

                    TOM
Don't come the little cunt with me.
I don't give a fuck. I been looking after
people in this area for longer than you
been alive.

There's a natural process been . . .
occurring here. Whereby the people
who are going about their business
come to me for a service and I, I'm,
I fulfil that. And then one day out of
nowhere, fuckers like you, you see, you
cut through all these strands that keep
the economic . . . organism . . . you
stab it in the heart. Yes. You do. And
it's happened before. And Jim and Tony
and other people, and me, we have to
patch that up. We have to make sure
that . . . We have to re-establish a
certain balance. A delicate fucking
process.

Do you understand?

                    GIT
I didn't know anything about . . .
what . . . you're saying.

                    TOM
And that's my fault. I'm saying that
now. It is. It's my business to make a
certain awareness . . . happen.

And obviously there's a weakness in
the system. We've got to find that cog
and oil it. And oil it properly.

And let's get going again. Do you
know?

Now there's a certain amount of repair
to be done. Okay? And you have to do
it from within the system. In other

134

words, you don't work unless you work
for me. Nobody does. All else is chaos
otherwise. You work for me, to a
certain . . . thing . . . where everything
is happening together. It's not 'Ah, I'm
just gonna do this thing over here,
because I feel like it . . . ' Because
then, over here, there's some other
eejit doing some other old shit, that's
against . . . you know? Okay?

Pause.

GIT
So what . . . do you . . . want me to do?

TOM
Well you've already placed *yourself* in a
certain position. 'I'm out here. I'm
taking risks.' That's revealed things
about what I think indicates things that
you're prepared to do. You know?

So I'm giving you something to do for
me. And this should make things,
alright, then, you see?

Short pause.

Now. Crude details.

TOM takes some paper from the desk.

Over the years I've let go of some
things that were just becoming fucking
trials. I'm sure you know what I mean.
Small things. Not worth getting upset
about, but Jesus they're mounting up.
And one day you find 'I am upset. I'm
after letting this fester into something
that now I'm either gonna go insane
about it or I'm just . . . just have to
leave it now' . . .

These are those type of things. Things
which I've preferred to forget about.
Too much trouble. 'I don't have the
time. It's not *worth* it' . . . Whatever.
These are uncollected debts. Debts
which I chose to write off. But which
are still outstanding and, legitimately,
collectable.

And I want you to get them.

135

Pause.

> This first one. And this is where you'll
> see I'm being reasonable.

TOM hands GIT a sheet of paper.

> Garrett Freely, that man owes me four
> and a half grand. Now I know that
> Garrett Freely will never *see* four and
> a half grand, let alone be able to pay
> it back – you get me one and a half,
> I'll be more than happy. This one.
> Ha hah . . .

TOM hands GIT a sheet of paper.

> Shamey Keating, you see, another . . .
> little fucking . . . He owes me, *all* he
> owes me is twelve hundred quid. And
> he has it, he's got quite a successful
> little business, that man. But d' you
> see what I mean? I let it slide. It's six
> years old. It' s nearly too fucking
> embarrassing at this stage, you know?

TOM looks at a sheet of paper.

> And eh, this one. Well it might be too
> ambitious just yet. But we' ll see how
> you go. You understand all of this now,
> this is the repair. I'm getting what you
> cost me. You get to atone for all the
> messing. And the cogs, you know? The
> machine is . . .

> And don't make us come looking for
> you. 'Cause we'll fucking murder you.
> We'll fucking kill you.

22   INT. DAY

SYLVESTER HEAVEY'S workshop. It is quiet. GIT sits at a bench. ANTO
sits near him. Just watching GIT. GIT stares at the bench. He is scared.
SYLVESTER puts a cup of tea in front of GIT.

> SYL
> Hold on.

SYLVESTER goes to a press and takes a bottle of whiskey. He pours a large
shot into GIT'S cup and takes a mug. Pouring a shot for ANTO.

> GIT
> I mean I couldn't fucking hardly
> understand what he was saying. He

136

was like one of these mad . . . dictators
or something.

SYL

Drink your tea.

SYL looks at the two sheets of paper TOM gave GIT.

ANTO

What'll we do, Syl?

SYL

Garrett Freely. Used to run a business
renting slot machines. This right at the
onslaught of video games. Sank
everything he had into the slots.

Man's an idiot. Drinks up in the
Willows. Alcoholic.

He wouldn't even have fifty quid at a
time, boys.

Tom French is sending you after thin
air, there.

ANTO

Why?

Pause.

SYL

I'd say one of three reasons. A, and
hope this is it, he's giving youse a pain
in the arse and hoping you'll get too
scared to go back empty-handed. In
which case you'll go away and never
come back. Or B, this is sort of a way
of selling you the debts. You owe the
money now and you're more likely to
get it for him. That's not too good a
situation. Or C, and this 'd be the
worst, (Pause) I'm looking at this:
Shamey Keating. (Pause) Shamey
Keating's a hard cunt, bookie. I don't
think youse could handle his boys. You
go round there looking for money.
Phhh . . . You're fucked, (Short pause)
in my opinion. So C could be, he's
getting you fucked, and getting it done
for him, while giving Keating a bit of
aggravation.

ANTO.
What do you think we should do?

SYL
I think you should impress the living
shit out of Tom French. Make him see
that you're committed to making
amends. And maybe he won't send you
after Keating. And maybe he won't
send you after whoever the third one
is. Because I'll bet youse a grand it'll
be miles out of your league. And right
now, you need to take care of *only the
shit you can handle.* (Short pause.)
'Cause God only knows what's after
that.

4   Alternative Friendly Face Scene from Unrevised Third Draft.

An Alternative Confrontation with the Hitman

EXT. BACK OF THE HOUSE DUSK

The MAN and GIT come out. FRANK sits in the back of the car with the door open. JIM leans against the car. They stand around uncomfortably. FRANK looks at the MAN as though he is a complete stranger. The MAN nods a greeting.

> JIM
> How's it going?

> MAN (nods)
> Yeah.

> FRANK (from car)
> I' m sorry but I have no idea who the hell you are.

> MAN
> Yeah, what's happened is the fella who was originally . . . meant to come down he's . . . eh, he hasn't been able to get down.

> FRANK
> Who was it?

> MAN
> I'm sorry, I wouldn't . . . I don't know who it was supposed to be.

Pause.

No one quite knows how to handle this.

> JIM
> Well, you can understand, that we're in a situation now, that we have this man that we're supposed to give to someone who *knows* him. Now that's not happening, is it?

The MAN shrugs.

> MAN
> Well, there's nothing I can do about that. I mean what do you want?

JIM looks at GIT as if to say "What do you think?'

GIT shakes his head slightly.

> JIM (producing gun)
> I want you to put your fucking hands
> on your head because I'm a bit tired of
> this.

INT. HOUSE NIGHT

This is the room with the tarpaulin spread over the floor. The MAN sits
bound to a chair. The others are in the room. FRANK is bound and sitting
on the floor. JIM and GIT stand over the MAN. JIM holds a big knife.

> JIM
> What's this for?

> MAN
> I don't know. It was just here.

Pause.

> GIT
> Why have you got the whole floor
> covered with this?

GIT kicks the tarpaulin.

> MAN
> I don't know, that was just here as well,
> I kind of slept on it.

> GIT
> That's bullshit, isn't it? You put it
> down.

> FRANK
> For wrapping me up.

> JIM
> Would you be quiet, and leave this to
> us, okay? Thank you.

> FRANK
> I've been vindicated. I'm entitled to
> give my opinion. You might listen to
> me in the future now.

> JIM
> You'll be entitled to get back into that
> fucking boot in a minute, if you don't
> be quiet.

> FRANK
> Ah now, here, no way . . .

140

                         GIT
            Frank, that's enough. Please. Thank
            you. Thanks, that's enough, alright?

                        FRANK
            But you're not listen . . .

                         GIT
            That's enough!

Pause.

                 GIT (attention back on MAN)
            See there's . . . a problem with what
            you're telling us. If he wasn't gonna
            recognise you. What was the point of
            you coming down? How was that
            supposed to reassure him? (Pause) Do
            you see what I'm talking about?

                        FRANK
            Yeah, exactly.

                         GIT
            Frank . . . (To MAN) D'you see what I
            mean? Cause we don't want to hurt
            you. But we really need some help,
            here.

The MAN nods.

                         GIT
            Okay?

Pause.

                         MAN
            I was supposed to go down with yous
            from here. Leave it to yous to find him.
            You get into trouble, it's not gonna cost
            anybody anything. You take care a
            business, I take care of him.

                        FRANK
            Just like that, yeah?

FRANK struggles to his feet, leaning against the wall.

                         MAN
            And then . . . yous are late and . . .

                         GIT
            What d'you mean take care of him?

                         141

                    MAN
            You know . . . look after him.

                    GIT
            Look after him? Take care of him . . .

Pause.

                    GIT
            You mean kill him?

                    MAN
            Whatever.

                    GIT
            So why are we here? (Indicates himself
            and JIM)

                    MAN
            What do you mean?

                    GIT
            I mean, besides being the fucking
            eejits, what's our part in this?

Pause.

                    MAN
            Did yous not get it?

Pause.

                    GIT

            Get what?

                    MAN
            The money. (Short pause) For the
            plates.

Pause. GIT and JIM look around. FRANK is gone.

Above: Sabrina Bradley (Antoine Byrne) and Git Hynes (Peter McDonald)
Below: Bunny Kelly (Brendan Gleeson) and Git Hynes (Peter McDonald)

Above: Bunny Kelly (Brendan Gleeson)

Below: Git Hynes (Peter McDonald) and Frank Grogan (Peter Caffrey)

Above (left to right): Friendly Face (Donal O'Kelly), Frank Grogan (Peter Caffrey) Git Hynes (Peter McDonald) and Bunny Kelly (Brendan Gleeson)

Below: Git Hynes (Peter McDonald) and 'Girlfriend' (Rachel Brady)

Above: Bunny Kelly (Brendan Gleeson) and Git Hynes (Peter McDonald)
review the bodies of Frank Grogan (Peter Caffrey) and Tom French (Tony Doyle)

Below: Sabrina Bradley (Antoine Byrne) and Bunny Kelly (Brendan Gleeson)

CAST AND CREW CREDITS

BBC FILMS
BORD SCANNÁN NA HÉIREANN
IRISH FILM BOARD
presents in association with
RADIO TEILIFÍS EIREANN

EUSKAL MEDIA

A TREASURE FILMS PRODUCTION

I WENT DOWN

Brendan Gleeson
Peter McDonald
Peter Caffrey
Tony Doyle

Casting   Deirdre O'Kane
Costume Designer   Kathy Strachan
Production Designer   Zoe MacLeod
Editor   Emer Reynolds
Music composed by   Dario Marianelli
Director of Photography   Cian de Buitléar

Executive Producers
Mark Shivas
David Collins
Rod Stoneman

Produced by
Robert Walpole

Written by
Conor McPherson

Directed by
Paddy Breathnach

Cast (*in order of appearance*)

Git Hynes ....Peter McDonald
Sabrina Bradley ....Antoine Byrne
Anto ....David Wilmot
Johnner Doyle ....Michael McElhatton
Bunny Kelly ....Brendan Gleeson
Steo Gannon ....Joe Gallagher
Tom French ....Tony Doyle
Little Boy at Teresa's ....Liam Regan
Petrol Station Attendant ....Kevin Hely
Cork Barman ....Eamonn Hunt
Cork Man 1 ....Frank O'Sullivan
Cork Man 2 ....Jason Byrne
Cork Man 3 ....Eamon A. Kelly
Frank Grogan ....Peter Caffrey
Caroline ....Carly Baker
Teresa ....Carmel Callan
Caroline's Mum ....Margaret Callan
Garda ....Denis Conway
The Friendly Face ....Donal O'Kelly
Receptionist ....Amelia Crowley
Loser in Nightclub ....Conor McPherson
Git's Girlfriend ....Rachel Brady
Bunny's Girlfriend ....Anne Kent
Sonny Mulligan ....Johnny Murphy
Young Frank ....Don Wycherley
Young Tom ....John Bergin

Crew Credits

Script Executive BBC Films .Stephanie Guerrasio

1st Assistant Director . . . . .Lisa Mulcahy

Sound Recordist . . . . .Simon J. Willis

Second Unit Director . . . . . . .John Erraught

Production Accountant . . . . . .David Sheehy

Production Manager . . . . . . .Maggie Mooney

Script Supervisor . . . . .Tasha Chapman

Boom Operator . . . . .Noel Quinn

Cable Puller . . . . .Conor O'Toole

Sound Trainee . . . . .Eoin Holohan

Focus Puller . . . . .Conor Kelly

Clapper Loader . . . . .Simon Walsh

Camera Trainee . . . . .Eoin Keating

Camera Grip . . . . .Joe Quigley

Assistant Grip . . . . .Wally O'Sullivan

Art Director . . . . .Tom McCullagh

Assistant Art Director . . . . .Niamh Barry

Storyboard Artist . . . . .Romek Delimata

Art Department Handler . . . . . . .Big Malkie

Props Buyer . . . . .Carmel O'Connor

Draftsman . . . . .Alan Gilmore

Props Maker . . . . .Brian Buckley

Property Master . . . . .Dave Peters

Stand-by Prop . . . . .Pat McKane

Trainee Stand-by Prop . . . . .Stephen Mac Avin

Dressing Prop . . . . .Eoin Lewis

Trainee Dressing Prop . . . . .John Porter

2nd Assistant Director . . . . .Mary Gough

3rd Assistant Director . . . . .Maria O'Connor

Trainee Assistant Director . . . . . . .Nell Wright

Trainee Assistant Director . . . .Dermot Whelan

Additional Trainee Assistant Directors

Clodagh Tierney

Glenn Delaney

Second Unit Lighting Cameraman .Seamus Deasy

Camera Operator . . . . .Eamon De Buitléar

Camera Operator . . . . .Seamus Corcoran

Focus Puller . . . . .Ivan Meagher

Focus Puller . . . . .Keith Durham

Clapper Loader . . . . .Shane Deasy

Clapper Loader . . . . .Adrienne Dollard

Trainee Clapper Loader . . . . .Grainne O'Kane

Trainee Script Supervisor . . . . .Sabine Wuhrer

Stills Photographer . . . . .Jonathan Hession

Unit Manager . . . . .Luke Johnston

Location Manager . . . . .Dermot Cleary

Location Assistant . . . . .Liz Kenny

Location Trainee . . . . .Fiona Hunt

Production Co-ordinator .Anneliese O'Callaghan

Asst Production Co-ordinator . .Niamh O'Dea

Production Trainee . . . . .Barbara Flood

Assistant to Director . . . . . .Bernice Burnside

Assistant Accountant . . . . . .Geraldine Nolan

Casting Co-ordinator . . . . . . .Fiona McGarry

Wardrobe Supervisor . . . . .Sheila Fahey

Wardrobe Assistant . . . . .Fiona Whelan

Make-Up Artist . . . . .Debbie Boylan

Trainee Make Up . . . . .Fiona Hogan

Claire Lambe

Mandy Kierrans

Hairdresser . . . . .Anne Dunne

Assistant Hairdresser . . . . .Carole Dunne

Trainee Hairdresser . . . . .Muriel Bell

Gaffer .Tony Swan

Best Boy . . . . .James Maguire

Electrician . . . . .Jim Farrell

Electrician / Generator Operator . .Davy Mayes

Special Effects Supervisor . . . . .Maurice Foley

Special Effects . . . . .Brendan Walsh

Marty Kelly

Michael Doyle

Graham Bushe

Armourer . . . . .John McKenna

Stunt Co-ordinator . . . . .Phillipe Zone

Stuntman . . . . .Eamon A. Kelly

Rigger . . . . .Terence Wellings

Standby Painter . . . . .Gary O'Donnell

Standby Carpenter . . . . . . .Eddie Humphries

Construction Manager . . . . .Gerry Drew

Chargehand Painter . . . . .Sean Scott

Painter . . . . .Thomas Lundy Jnr

Chargehand Carpenter . . . . . . .Richard Phelan

Carpenter . . . . .Eamon Hill

Carpenter . . . . .Brian Molloy

Stagehand . . . . .Gerard McGrath

Stagehand . . . . .Richard Devlin

Plasterer . . . . .James Irwin

Unit Publicist .Ginger Corbett, Corbett & Keene

EPK Camera . . . . .Liam McGrath

EPK Sound . . . . .Kelly-Anne O'Neill

Unit Nurse . . . . .Liz McGarry

Caterers . . . . .Fitzers Catering

Action Vehicle Coordinator . . . . . . .Liam Kelly

Artiste/ Unit Car . . . . .Peadar Gaffney

Artiste Car . . . . .Paul Cullen

Minibus . . . . .Gerry McIlroy

Prop Truck/Standby Vehicle . . . . . .Pat Kirwan

Prop Truck (Runaround/Dressing)

Niall O'Huadhaigh